Corrective Reading

Series Guide

Siegfried Engelmann • **Susan Hanner** • **Gary Johnson**

**SRA
McGraw-Hill**

Columbus, Ohio

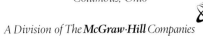

A Division of The McGraw·Hill Companies

Acknowledgments

The authors of SRA's *Corrective Reading* programs are Siegfried Engelmann and others, including Wes Becker, Linda Carnine, Julie Eisele, Phyllis Haddox, Susan Hanner, Gary Johnson, Linda Meyer, Jean Osborn, and Steve Osborn.

Photo Credits

Cover Photos: (tl, tcl, tcr, bcl, br bcr) KS Studios: (tr, bl,) ©David Madison Photography.

SRA/McGraw-Hill

A Division of The McGraw·Hill Companies

Send all inquiries to:
SRA/McGraw-Hill
8787 Orion Place
Columbus, Ohio 43240-4027

ISBN 0-02-674837-1

9 10 DBH 04 03

Contents

Contents continued

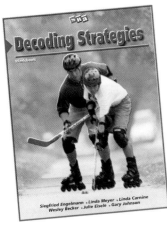

A teacher doesn't want to give up on children who seem destined to fail because they have difficulty reading. But even the most talented teachers are stopped by reading programs that leave students lagging behind their peers no matter how much effort both teacher and students pour into them.

With *Corrective Reading,* a teacher doesn't have to face that frustration again . . . and a student need never be doomed to a lifetime of poor reading—and poor learning.

Corrective Reading

For those abandoned by traditional approaches . . .

Forty percent of all nine–year-olds score below the "Basic" level on the **National Assessment of Educational Progress (NAEP).** Reading failure is the overwhelming reason for children being retained or assigned to special education.

Without help, these children never catch up. Instead, they spend years struggling, being left further behind.

Corrective Reading offers a proven solution

For many children like these, *Corrective Reading's* tightly structured instructional method is the answer.

Numerous studies document the effectiveness of *Corrective Reading*. An overview of research on *Corrective Reading* established that percentile scores for students in the program increase rather than remain at the same level and that the slope of their learning line is sharply steeper than expected.

In Lee County, Alabama, at-risk 4th graders improved 10.5 percentile points, against the district average loss of −3.5 percentile points. Eighty percent of these students moved out of the at-risk category.

DiChiara, 1997

Even nonreaders have been brought to grade level–some in less than two years

Corrective Reading is a complete core program that uses the groundbreaking Direct Instruction method to help students master the essential decoding and comprehension skills they need not only to read well, but to learn well.

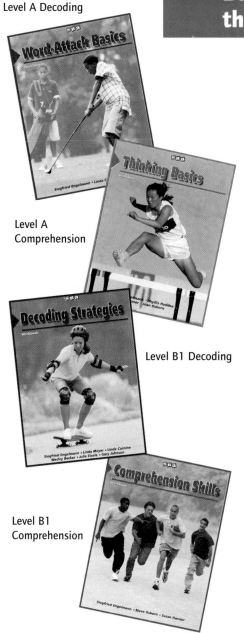

Level A Decoding

Level A Comprehension

Level B1 Decoding

Level B1 Comprehension

Direct Instruction combines three distinctive elements:

1 A carefully developed and tested program design structured so that students learn how to learn as they master increasingly complex skills and strategies.

2 A scripted presentation approach that uses a brisk pace, carefully chosen exercises and examples, and other special presentation techniques to engage even reluctant learners.

3 Complete learning materials, including student books, workbooks, and teacher presentation books and guides that provide everything from placement tests to a management system that rewards hard work. This system helps change student attitudes about reading.

In a climate where accountability has never counted more, Corrective Reading is carefully structured to ensure success

Despite teachers' best efforts, traditional reading programs fail some students. One low achieving or underachieving reader may fail to develop a basic skill, such as how to sound out an unknown word. Another may have trouble remembering written information. Still others may not recognize words quickly and effortlessly to process text and transform words into meaning. As these students get left behind, reading becomes a punishing task. Students may become class clowns. Or they may become indifferent, even disruptive.

Corrective Reading's proven methods can rescue:

- Students who cannot read accurately and fluently

- Students with attention deficits

- Students whose overall academic performance is hurt by poor comprehension

- Students whose reading is putting them at risk of failure

> *In Texas, 4th–6th-grade urban minority students using **Corrective Reading** gained 1.6 months per month of instruction in total reading scores, compared with just .8 months per month of instruction for all other Chapter 1 students in the same district. The **Corrective Reading** group also saw vocabulary increases more than three times greater than their other Chapter 1 schoolmates.*
>
> *Vitale, Medland, Romance and Weaver, 1993*

Every student with a reading problem deserves Corrective Reading

As more and more such failures fuel the accountability movement, teachers and administrators are increasingly turning to Corrective Reading.

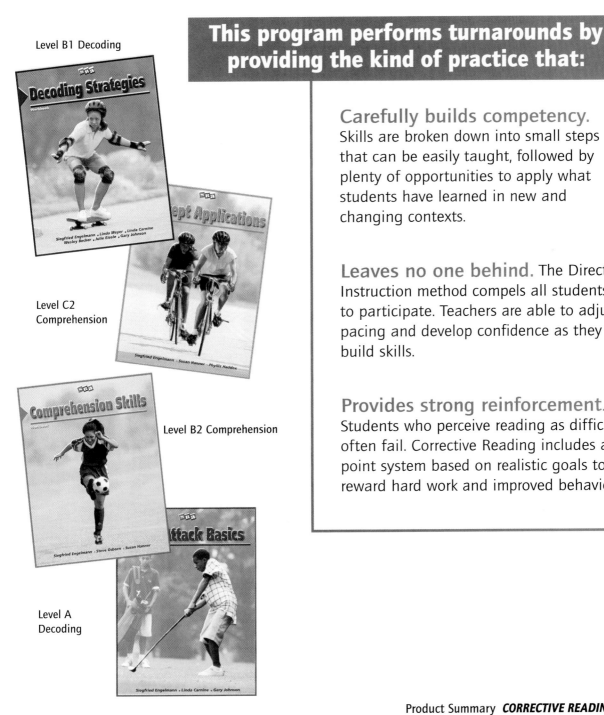

Level B1 Decoding

Level C2 Comprehension

Level B2 Comprehension

Level A Decoding

This program performs turnarounds by providing the kind of practice that:

Carefully builds competency.
Skills are broken down into small steps that can be easily taught, followed by plenty of opportunities to apply what students have learned in new and changing contexts.

Leaves no one behind. The Direct Instruction method compels all students to participate. Teachers are able to adjust pacing and develop confidence as they build skills.

Provides strong reinforcement.
Students who perceive reading as difficult often fail. Corrective Reading includes a point system based on realistic goals to reward hard work and improved behavior.

Start where students are. End where they need to be

Whatever students' difficulties and whatever their reading level, *Corrective Reading* allows teachers to structure a program that can meet their needs. With two major strands and four instructional levels, it can address a wide range of reading problems.

Students can work on decoding skills, comprehension skills, or both. Placement tests included with the program let you determine where your students should begin.

Choose Decoding, Comprehension, or both.

1 Decoding Programs

help students who have trouble identifying words, who don't understand how the arrangement of letters in a word relates to its pronunciation, and whose reading rate is inadequate.

2 Comprehension Programs

help readers who do not follow instructions well, lack vocabulary and background knowledge needed to understand what they read, and have poor thinking skills.

Level A

Word Attack Basics
Decoding A

Decoding A teaches nonreaders sound-spelling relationships explicitly and systematically, and shows students how to sound out words.

Students are first taught the connection between sound-spelling relationships through regularly spelled words. Then irregular words are introduced. Later, sentence- and story-reading activities are used to teach students to apply their newly learned strategies in real contexts.

After completing Decoding A, students can be expected to read basic sentences and simple stories composed mostly of regularly spelled words. They can accurately read many words that typically confuse poor readers, and can read quickly enough to comprehend what they read.

Thinking Basics
Comprehension A

Comprehension A teaches basic reasoning skills that form the framework for learning information. It also fills in crucial gaps in students' background knowledge.

Students are taught thinking operations they can use to solve problems in any content area. They practice organizing groups of related facts and develop basic logic skills such as making inferences. They also learn common information they may be lacking, as well as word meanings.

At the end of Comprehension A, students are able to complete simple analogies, identify synonyms, recite poems, and follow simple instructions. They have mastered some higher-order thinking skills and established a foundation on which to build.

 in brief...

	1 Decoding **65 Lessons**	**2** Comprehension **60 Lessons**
For:	**Nonreaders or those in grades 3.5–12** who read so haltingly they can't understand what they read	**Poor comprehenders in grades 4–12** who cannot understand concepts underlying much of the material being taught
Teaches:	**Word-attack skills:** Phonemic awareness, sound-symbol identification, sounding out, regular and irregular words, sentence reading	**Thinking basics:** Deduction and induction, analogies, vocabulary, true/false, recitation, information (such as calendar skills)
Outcomes:	60 wpm, 98% accuracy, reading at about a 2.5 grade level	Some higher-order thinking skills and many word definitions

Level B

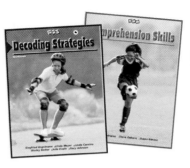

Decoding Strategies
Decoding B1 and B2

In **Decoding Levels B1** and **B2**, word-attack skills are refined and applied to more sound-spelling patterns and difficult words. These skills are applied in stories designed to correct mistakes the poor reader typically makes.

Students are introduced to new words and word types, phonemic relationships, long and short vowel sounds, new sound combinations, and new word endings. They apply their discrimination skills by reading stories of increasing length and with more complex syntax, then answering comprehension questions both orally and in writing.

After completing **Decoding B1** and **B2**, students show great improvement in both reading speed and accuracy.

Comprehension Skills
Comprehension B1 and B2

The **Comprehension B1** and **B2** programs teach the many separate skills necessary to read content area textbooks, learn new information, and respond to written questions that involve deductions and rule applications.

Lessons focus on developing the background knowledge, vocabulary, and thinking skills needed to construct meaning from written text. Reasoning and analysis strategies are taught in content-rich contexts, enabling students to transfer these strategies to many subject areas. Games help students master important facts and vocabulary.

By the time they finish the two level B programs, students have learned basic strategies that allow them to read for information in academic subjects and learn new facts and vocabulary.

 in brief...

	1 Decoding	**2** Comprehension
	B1: 65 Lessons – B2: 65 Lessons	**B1: 60 Lessons – B2: 65 Lessons**
For:	**Poor readers;** students in grades 3–12 who do not read at an adequate rate and who confuse words	**Poor reasoners in grades 4–12;** those who have difficulty with conclusions, contradictions, written directions
Teaches:	**Decoding strategies:** letter and word discrimination, sound and letter combinations, word endings, story reading, literal and inferential comprehension	**Comprehension skills:** more advanced reasoning, handling information, vocabulary, analyzing sentences, writing skills
Outcomes:	**B1:** 90 wpm, 98% accuracy, reading at about a 3.9 grade level; **B2:** 120 wpm, 98% accuracy, reading at about a 4.9 grade level	A variety of comprehension skills that can be applied in all school subjects; the ability to read information and learn new facts and vocabulary

Skill Applications
Decoding C

Decoding C bridges the gap between advanced word-attack skills and the ability to read textbooks and other informational material.

Students learn more than 500 new vocabulary words and read a variety of passages, from narrative to expository, with fairly sophisticated vocabulary. To prepare them to read in all content areas, Decoding C introduces sentence types and conventions that are typical of textbook material.

After completing Decoding C, students average 150 words a minute at 98 percent accuracy. They can read materials with a wide range of syntax, vocabulary, format, and content. They can learn new information and apply it after only one reading.

Concept Applications
Comprehension C

Comprehension C teaches students to use thinking skills independently. They move from basic reasoning tools to higher-order skills.

Students learn to infer definitions from context, read for basic information, write precise directions, recognize the main idea of a passage, draw conclusions from basic evidence, and identify contradictions and faulty arguments.

By the end of Comprehension C, students can evaluate advertisements and editorials, and recognize contradictory information in newspaper and magazine articles. They have learned to evaluate sources of information and know how to use information resources.

Level C in brief...

	1 Decoding **125 Lessons**	**2** Comprehension **140 Lessons**
For:	**Fair readers;** students in grades 4–12 who have trouble with multisyllabic words and typical textbook material	**Students in grades 6 and up** who can't comprehend sophisticated text, do not learn well from material they read, or have trouble thinking critically
Teaches:	**Skill applications:** additional sound combinations, affixes, vocabulary development, reading expository text, recall of events, sequencing, and building reading rate	**Concept applications:** organizing and operating on information, using sources of information, communicating information
Outcomes:	Over 150 wpm, reading at about a 7.0 grade level	Ability to apply analytical skills to real-life situations and answer literal and inferential questions based on passages read

Overview

SRA's *Corrective Reading* programs are divided into two strands:

1 Decoding

2 Comprehension

The diagram of the series shows the title and skill emphasis of each program. The diagram also indicates the number of lessons in each program. The number of lessons is an indication of the approximate number of school days the students need to complete each program.

Decoding A

65 lessons

Emphasizes basic reading skills: sounds, rhyming, pronunciation, sounding out, word reading, sentence reading, story reading, rate building, workbook applications

Comprehension A

5 preprogram lessons
60 regular lessons
7 Fact Game lessons

Emphasizes oral language skills: deductions, inductions, analogies, vocabulary building, inferences, recitation behavior, common information

Decoding B1

65 lessons

Emphasizes pronunciation, critical letter and word discriminations, letter combinations, word reading, accurate story reading, comprehension questions, rate building, workbook applications

Comprehension B1

60 regular lessons
12 Fact Game/
Mastery Test lessons

Emphasizes literal and inferential skills, reading for information, writing skills, following sequenced instructions, analyzing contradictions, learning information

Decoding B2

65 lessons

Emphasizes pronunciation, letter combinations, word discriminations, word reading, accurate story reading, comprehension questions, rate building, workbook applications

Comprehension B2

65 regular lessons
7 Fact Game/
Mastery Test lessons

Emphasizes literal and inferential skills, reading for information, writing skills, following sequenced instructions, analyzing contradictions, learning information

Decoding C

125 lessons

Emphasizes letter combinations, affixes, vocabulary development, accurate story reading, informational reading, comprehension questions, rate building, workbook applications

Comprehension C

140 regular lessons
9 Fact Game/
Mastery Test lessons

Emphasizes critical thinking skills in analyzing arguments, organizing and utilizing information, using sources of information, communicating information

Features of the Series

SRA's *Corrective Reading* programs have features that have been demonstrated through research studies to be effective in improving student performance.

◆ Each program is a core program, not ancillary material. Each program contains all the material you need and provides students with all the practice they need to learn the skills.

◆ All skills and strategies are taught through DIRECT INSTRUCTION. This approach is the most efficient for communicating with the students, for evaluating their performance on a moment-to-moment basis, and for achieving student mastery. Students are not simply exposed to skills—skills are taught.

◆ Students are taught everything that is required for what they are to do later. Also, they are not taught skills that are not needed for later skill applications. The programs concentrate only on the necessary skills, not the nuances.

◆ Each program is based on cumulative skill development. Skills and strategies are taught, with lots of examples. Once a skill or strategy is taught, students receive practice in applying that skill until the end of the program. This type of cumulative development has been demonstrated by research studies to be the most effective method for teaching skills so that they become well learned or automatic.

◆ Because of the cumulative development of skills, the difficulty of material increases gradually but steadily.

◆ Each program is divided into daily lessons that usually can be presented in a class period (35–45 minutes of teacher-directed work and independent student applications).

◆ Each program provides detailed data on student performance. Students see documentation of their improvement as they progress through the program.

◆ Each program includes an effective management system. Students earn points for performance on each part of the daily lesson. Records of this performance may be used for awarding grades and documenting progress in specific skill areas.

◆ Each program specifies both teacher and student behavior. The lessons are scripted. The scripts specify what you do and say as well as appropriate student responses. The scripted lessons assure that you will (a) use uniform wording, (b) present examples in a manner that communicates effectively with students, and (c) be able to complete a lesson during a class period.

◆ The placement tests are administered individually and are designed to measure relevant skills. The Decoding Placement Test measures each student's decoding accuracy and rate of oral reading. The Comprehension Placement Test measures performance on analogies, similarities, recitation behavior, deductions, and other skills assumed in complex comprehension activities.

Each program is designed to be used independently. Students may be placed at the beginning of one program and complete all lessons in that program. The programs may also be used in either a single-strand sequence or a double-strand sequence.

A single-strand sequence places students in one strand (Decoding, for example), and the students move through the strand from the point of initial placement (**Decoding A, B1, B2, or C)** to the end of the strand (**Decoding C**).

The double-strand sequence requires that students receive two full periods of instruction each day—one period in a Decoding program and one period in a Comprehension program. Once students are placed in a Decoding program, they may be placed in a Comprehension program that *is at either the same level or a lower level than the Decoding program*. For example, students might be placed in **Decoding B1** and **Comprehension B1,** two programs at the same level, or they might be placed in **Decoding B1** and **Comprehension A**, where the comprehension placement is lower than the decoding placement.

The sequence of reading vocabulary used in the Comprehension programs parallels that in the Decoding programs. Students decode the independent workbook material in the **Comprehension B1** program better if they already have mastered the skills taught in the **Decoding B1** program.

The Materials

The teacher's materials for each level of *Corrective Reading* consist of a *Teacher's Guide* and one (or two) *Teacher Presentation Book. The Teacher's Guide* contains basic information about the program and specific information for presenting exercises and correcting mistakes. The *Teacher's Guide* also includes a copy of a placement test, a Scope and Sequence Chart, a list of Behavioral Objectives, and a Skills Profile Chart.

The *Teacher Presentation Books* contain a script for each lesson. Scripts specify what you say and do and how students are to respond.

The *Teacher Presentation Books* also include reproductions of the student pages with answers.

All levels of *Corrective Reading* have a consumable student *Workbook* that contains activities for each lesson. Some activities are teacher directed; others are independent. All *Workbook* activities are integral parts of the lessons. The *Workbook* also contains charts on which students record points earned for their performance on the parts of each lesson.

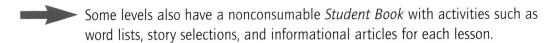 Some levels also have a nonconsumable *Student Book* with activities such as word lists, story selections, and informational articles for each lesson.

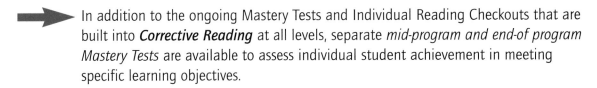 In addition to the ongoing Mastery Tests and Individual Reading Checkouts that are built into *Corrective Reading* at all levels, separate *mid-program and end-of program Mastery Tests* are available to assess individual student achievement in meeting specific learning objectives.

Decoding Programs 1999	Teacher's Guide	Teacher Presentation Books	Consumable Workbook	Nonconsumable Student Book	Supplemental Mastery Test
Decoding A	1	2	1		1 pkg.
Decoding B1	1	1	1	1	1 pkg.
Decoding B2	1	1	1	1	1 pkg.
Decoding C	1	2	1	1	1 pkg.
Comprehension Programs 1999					
Comprehension A	1	2	1		1 pkg.
Comprehension B1	1	1	1		1 pkg.
Comprehension B2	1	1	1		1 pkg.
Comprehension C	1	2	1	1	1 pkg.

The Programs

SRA's *Corrective Reading* programs are designed to help a wide range of students in grades 3 through 12. The programs are designed to meet the needs of students who are performing below grade-level expectations in reading, and perhaps other subjects, too. Some students will require a great deal of remedial work; other students will have far fewer skill deficiencies. The goals of the Level A programs, which deal with very basic skills, are relatively modest in number, while the objectives of the Level C programs are manifold. Students who initially are placed in a Level C program have mastered the basics and are ready to master a wider range of skills.

The programs are appropriate for students who speak and understand basic conversational English and whose scores on the *Corrective Reading* Decoding Placement Test or Comprehension Placement Test indicate that they belong in one of the programs. The programs are not meant to be used with students who do not speak English, or whose grasp of English is quite weak.

The programs work effectively with students who would traditionally be identified as learning disabled, educationally handicapped, or perceptually handicapped. As long as students demonstrate the skill level necessary to enter a program, they may be placed in that program.

▶ The Decoding Programs

Below is a diagram of the four Decoding programs in SRA's *Corrective Reading* series.

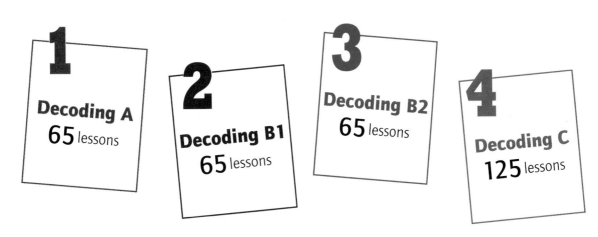

1 Decoding A 65 lessons

2 Decoding B1 65 lessons

3 Decoding B2 65 lessons

4 Decoding C 125 lessons

► *Introduction to the 1999 Edition*

The 1999 edition of the Decoding programs has a number of changes designed to make the teacher material easier for teachers to use and the student materials more attractive for students. Some program design changes address problems students experienced in the 1988 edition.

One major change in Decoding B1 has to do with the redesign of the early lessons in the program. The revision focused on the problems experienced by students who passed the placement test criteria to enter **Decoding B1** but did not go through the **Decoding A** program. A fair percentage of these students were able to read whole words but had no understanding of the relationship between letters and the sounds they usually make. These students floundered in the early lessons of **Decoding B1**. Through their teacher's persistence and the tasks that required that students respond to letter sounds, these students finally acquired understanding of letter-sound relationships.

The 1999 edition of Decoding B1 has beginning lessons that are far less laborious in teaching letter-sound relationships that these students haven't learned. The first ten lessons of the program provide a strong focus on sounds in isolation and identifying the sounds that specific letters make in words. Students also read sentences that contain word types that they are learning. By Lesson 11, they have a sufficiently solid basis in letter-sound relationships to learn sound combinations and to read stories composed of the words they have studied.

Changes in the 1999 edition of Decoding B2 focused on the problems experienced by students who passed the placement test criteria to enter **Decoding B2** but did not go through the **Decoding B1** program. Many of these students did not know all of the sound combinations (such as **ir, ou, ar, ea, igh, oul**) that are taught in the **Decoding B1** program. These students frequently made many word-reading errors, particularly on words that contain sound combinations, in the early lessons of **Decoding B2**. Sound-combination review exercises are provided in Lessons 1, 2, and 3 of the 1999 edition of **Decoding B2**.

Another skill that was difficult for students who started **Decoding B2** but did not go through the **Decoding B1** program is rewriting words that have endings (**striped, jogged**) without those endings (**stripe, jog**). Additional prompts were added to the early lessons in **Decoding B2** to better teach this skill.

Finally, some stories that begin in **Decoding B1** continue in **Decoding B2**. A story introduction is provided in the 1999 edition of **Decoding B2**.

▶ *The Decoding Programs and the Poor Decoder*

The Decoding programs are designed to change the behavior of the poor decoder. The specific decoding tendencies of this student suggest what a program must do to be effective in changing the student's behavior.

The poor decoder makes frequent word-identification errors.

The student makes a higher percentage of mistakes when reading connected sentences than when reading words in word lists. Often, the student reads words correctly in word lists and misidentifies the same words when they are embedded in connected sentences.

The specific mistakes the reader makes include word omissions, word additions, confusion of high-frequency words (such as **what** and **that**, **of** and **for**, **and** and **the**).

The student also reads synonyms (saying "pretty" for beautiful). The student often guesses at words, basing the guess on the word's beginning or ending. And the student is consistently inconsistent, making a mistake on one word in a sentence and then making a different mistake when re-reading the sentence.

The student doesn't seem to understand the relationship between the arrangement of letters in a word and the pronunciation of the word.

Often, the student is confused about the word meaning (a fact suggested by synonym reading, opposite reading, and word guessing). The strategy seems to be based on rules the student has been taught. The poor decoder follows such advice as: "Look at the beginning of the word and take a guess," "Think of what the word might mean," and "Look at the general shape of the word." The result is a complicated strategy that is often backwards: The student seems to think that to read a word one must first "understand" the word, then select the spoken word that corresponds to that understanding.

Although the poor decoder may use a strategy that is meaning based, the reader is often preempted from comprehending passages. The reason is that **the student doesn't read a passage with the degree of accuracy needed to understand what the passage actually says.** (Omitting the word **not** from one sentence changes the meaning dramatically.)

Furthermore, **the student's reading rate is often inadequate, making it difficult for the student to remember the various details of the passage, even if they were decoded accurately.** Often, the poor decoder doesn't have an effective reading comprehension strategy because the student's poor decoding and slow rate don't make the material sensible.

Finally, the poor decoder is not a highly motivated student. For this student, reading has been punishing. The student often professes indifference: "I don't care if I can read or not." But the student's behavior gives strong suggestions that the student cares a great deal.

The student's ineffective reading strategies and negative attitudes about reading become more ingrained as the reader gets older. To overcome them requires a very careful program, one that systematically replaces the strategies with new ones and that provides lots and lots of practice.

The procedures that are used in the program derive directly from the difficulties that students have with particular tasks.

Based on the problems students have, we can identify two major levels of difficulty. The less difficult level is reading isolated words. The more difficult level is reading words that are in a connected sentence context.

- *Isolated words* are easier because they do not prompt the student to use inappropriate guessing strategies that the student applies when reading connected sentences. When the student reads word lists, therefore, the student is not as likely to guess on the basis of the order of the preceding words, or on the basis of images that are prompted by preceding words. Not all word lists are the same level of difficulty.

- *Less difficult lists* require reading words that have similar parts. *More difficult lists* require reading words that do not have similar parts. This type of list is sometimes called a "mixed list" because all types of words appear in it.

- *Reading words in connected sentences* is more difficult than reading words in isolation. The task of reading a particular passage can be made relatively more difficult or less difficult.

- *Passage reading* is less difficult if the student has read the passage and received feedback on all errors.

- *Passage reading* is more difficult if the student is reading the passage for the first time.

LESSONS in *Corrective Reading* are designed to give students practice that leads them to become stronger in what is easier for them to do and that gives them progressive practice in the more difficult reading endeavors. The lessons do this while remaining within the skill limits of the student, which means that an appropriately placed student will not be overwhelmed with difficult tasks or bored by tasks that are too easy.

EACH LESSON presents words in isolation and gives students practice with easier lists and more difficult lists. When new words are introduced, they often appear in lists of words that have similar parts. In later lessons, these same words appear in mixed lists where the students must rely more on the decoding skills taught earlier. Except for the early lessons in Level A, all lessons provide students with practice in reading familiar words in sentence contexts.

THE PROCEDURES require the students to read sentences or passages and then re-read them. In Levels B1, B2, and C, students keep error data on their individual second reading and on the first reading, called "reading checkouts." The lower errors on the second reading provide students with evidence that they are learning. Their improved performance on the first reading provides further evidence of their ability to retain and apply the decoding skills they have been taught.

THE STRUCTURE of the lessons addresses the student's skill deficiencies directly but positively, in a manner that provides the type of practice students need to relearn fundamental strategies and to learn new skills, and that does not overwhelm them with material or rules that result in a high rate of errors.

▶ *The Problems*

An effective corrective reading program must address the specific needs of the poor decoder.

1 The learner must learn to look at the order of letters in a word and learn that this order suggests the general pronunciation of the word. Furthermore, the student must learn that the game is simple: first figure out how the letters suggest to say the word. Then see if the word you say is one that you recognize, one that has meaning. (Note that this strategy is basically the opposite of the one the typical poor decoder uses.)

2 The poor decoder must receive practice in reading connected sentences that are composed of words that have been taught in isolation. Merely because the student reads words in lists does not imply transfer to written sentences.

3 The student must receive strong reinforcement for working on reading because the task is very difficult and frustrating for the student. The student has received a great deal of evidence that reading is a puzzle that seems to be unsolvable.

4 Finally, the student must receive practice in reading a variety of passages. If the student practices reading only narrative passages, the student will not automatically transfer the reading skills to textooks, articles, or other forms of expository writing. Therefore, different styles must be introduced.

▶ *The Solutions*

SRA's *Corrective Reading* Decoding programs are successful with the poor decoder because they provide the careful integration, the practice, and the management details that the student needs to succeed.

The student receives daily practice in oral reading, with immediate feedback. (Only through oral reading can we discover what the student is actually reading.)

The student reads word lists with information about how to pronounce various letter combinations (such as **th** and **or**). The student also reads sentences and passages composed of words that have been taught. The sentences and passages are designed so they are relatively easy if the student approaches words as entities that are to be analyzed according to the arrangement of letters, but difficult if the student guesses on the basis of the context or syntax of the sentence. (The sentences are designed so that guesses often lead to identification of the wrong word.)

The Mastery Tests and checkouts in the Decoding programs assure that the student observes progress in reading rate and reading accuracy.

The Decoding programs present comprehension items in a way that demonstrates the relationship between what is decoded and how it is to be understood. Initially, the comprehension activities are deliberately separated from the decoding activities so that the student's misconceptions about reading are not exaggerated. The comprehension activities, however, show the student that what is read is to be understood.

Finally, the Decoding programs address the poor decoder's low self-image. The programs are designed so the student can succeed in real reading tasks. Furthermore, a point system that is based on realistic performance goals assures that the reader who tries will succeed and will receive reinforcement for improved performance.

In summary, the programs use a two-pronged approach. Each level teaches effective reading skills to replace the student's ineffective approach to reading. Each level also contains an effective management system that turns students on to reading. This turn-on is not achieved by "seducing" the reader with entertaining topics but by rewarding the reader for steady improvement in reading performance.   The approach **works.**

▶ *Progress Through the Decoding Programs*

The programs are designed so that there is a careful progression of skill development from level to level.

There are **FOUR** entry points.

1 Students who begin at

Level A

should complete A and B1 in a school year
(a total of 130 lessons)

2 Students who begin at

Level B1

should complete B1 and B2 in a school year
(a total of 130 lessons)

3 Students who begin at

Level B2

should complete B2 and most of C
in a school year

4 Students who begin at

Level C

should complete C and additional
outside reading in a school year

A summary of the programs follows. For each program, the summary describes
(a) the reading behavior of students typically placed in that program,
(b) what is taught, and (c) what students should be able to do at the
end of the program.

▶ Decoding A Word-Attack Basics

Who It's For

Decoding A is appropriate for extremely poor readers in the second half of grade 3 through high school who virtually lack decoding skills. These students read so inaccurately and haltingly that they are prevented from comprehending what they read.

What Is Taught

The following skills are taught in **Decoding A.**

- ◆ Identifying the sounds of letters
- ◆ Sounding out words that are presented orally and then saying them fast
- ◆ Sounding out and identifying written words that are spelled regularly
- ◆ Decoding irregularly spelled words
- ◆ Reading words "the fast way"
- ◆ Reading sentences
- ◆ Reading short selections
- ◆ Spelling

Related skills such as matching, word completion (for example, rhyming), and symbol scanning are included in the student Workbooks.

The basic objective in **Decoding A** is to teach students that there are regularly spelled words, words that are pronounced by blending the sounds of the letters in them. Once students understand that the identification of a word is related to its spelling, irregularly spelled words, such as **said** and **what**, are introduced. These words are spelled one way but pronounced in a different, "irregular" way.

The sentence-reading exercises give students practice in reading words that are presented within a context. Usually, students who qualify for this program do not understand what decoding is. This problem is magnified when they try to read sentences. Usually, their sentence-reading strategy involves guessing based on the syntax or the position of words within the sentence. For instance, they guess that the first word is "the."

The objective of the sentence-reading activities is to retrain students in how to read words in sentences. Although work on isolated words (in lists) teaches word-attack skills, practice in reading sentences ensures that students apply these skills.

The sentences in this program are designed so that there is low probability of guessing a word correctly. If students guess the next word in a sentence on the basis of the preceding words, they most likely will be wrong. The low-probability feature provides students with consistent evidence that guessing is not effective. A guess equals a mistake; therefore, students quickly abandon the guessing approach and use the decoding skills being taught.

The story-reading exercises give students practice in decoding material similar to what they will encounter at the beginning of **Decoding B1** and in answering comprehension questions about what they have read.

Outcome Behavior

Upon completion of **Decoding A,** students should be able to do the following activities.

- Read sentences, such as **She was a master at planting trees.**
  These sentences are composed primarily of regularly spelled words (containing as many as six sounds).

- Read short selections, such as the following:

  Ten men got in a truck.
  They went to the creek and set up a tent.
  How can ten men fit in the tent?
  They can not.
  Six men will sleep under a tree.

- Read common irregular words, such as **what, was, do, said, to, of,** and **you,** with only infrequent errors.

- Read words that begin with difficult letter combinations, such as **st, bl, sl, fl, pl, sw, cl, tr,** and **dr.**

- Read words that end with difficult letter combinations, such as **nt, nd, st, ts, mp, ps, cks, ls, ms, th, er, ing, ers,** and **y.**

- Pronounce commonly confused word parts, such as the **k** sound in **trick,** the **e** sound in **set,** and the **s** ending sound in **mats, runs,** and **munches.**

- Spell simple words that have a clear sound-symbol relationship, including words that contain **th, wh, sh, ch,** and various other letter combinations.

- Independently perform various simple activities, such as matching sounds and completing words with missing letters.

▶ Decoding B1 Decoding Strategies

■ Who It's For

Decoding B1 is appropriate for most problem readers in grades 3 through 12. They guess at words. They have trouble reading words like **what**, **that**, **a**, and **the** when the words appear in a sentence context. They add or omit words. They often read synonyms for printed words and are generally inconsistent in their reading behavior (reading a word correctly one time and missing it the next time).

■ What Is Taught

The typical **Decoding B1** lesson is divided into four major parts.

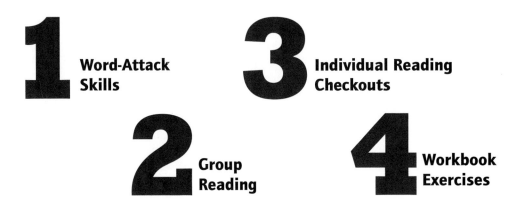

1 Word-Attack Skills

2 Group Reading

3 Individual Reading Checkouts

4 Workbook Exercises

Word-Attack Skills take up about 10 minutes of the period. Students practice pronouncing words, identifying the sounds of letters or letter combinations, and reading isolated words composed of sounds and sound combinations that they have learned. Students earn points for performance in the word-attack portion of the lesson.

Group Reading follows immediately after Word-Attack Skills. This part of the lesson takes approximately 15 to 20 minutes. Students take turns reading aloud from their Student Book. Students who are not reading follow along. The stories are divided into parts. If the group reads a part within the error limit, the teacher presents specified comprehension questions for the part.

Individual Reading Checkouts follow the Group Reading and take about 10 minutes. Assigned pairs of students read two passages. The first is from the lesson just read by the group; the second is from the preceding lesson. Each member of the pair first reads the passage from the current story, then the passage from the preceding lesson. A student can earn points for both passages. Points for the first passage are earned if the student reads within a specified error limit. To earn points for the second passage, the student must read the passage within a specified rate criterion and also a specified error criterion. (For instance, the student must read 85 words in 1 minute, with no more than 2 errors.)

Workbook Exercises are presented as the last part of the lesson. Some of these activities are teacher-directed and are very important to the students' skill development. Other activities are independent. The Workbook Exercises take about 10 minutes. Students earn points by staying within an error limit in the Workbook for the lesson.

The following activities are included in **Word-Attack Skills.**

- Pronouncing words with consonant blends **(slam, cast, flip)**, orally constructing words with endings (adding **ed** to **show** to pronounce **showed**), and identifying the component sounds of orally presented words

- Identifying the long and short sounds of the vowels **o, e, a,** and **i**

- Identifying the sounds of consonants

- Identifying the sounds of letter combinations **(th, ee, sh, or, ol, ch, wh, ing, er, oo, ea, oa, ai, ou, ar, oul, ir, igh, al)** and reading words with those combinations

- Reading lists of regularly spelled words, such as **mat** and **trip,** and irregularly spelled words, such as **what** and **said**

- Reading words that contain difficult consonant blends **(drop, splash, slip)**

- Reading words with endings **(dropping, rested)**

- Reading silent-**e** words **(save, times, hoped)**

- Reading compound words **(herself, anybody)**

- Practicing pattern drills that demonstrate consistent phonic relationships **(big, bag, beg, bug)**

The stories in **Decoding B1** increase in length, difficulty, and interest. All stories are composed of words that have been taught in the series or words that the students can already read. After new words and word types are introduced in the Word-Attack Activities, the words are incorporated in stories. Furthermore, the introduction of words in stories is cumulative, which means that once words have been introduced, they recur in the stories.

The syntax and structure of the stories are designed for the problem decoder and are designed to correct the mistakes the reader typically makes. Early stories are "low-interest" stories because the poor reader must concentrate on a new game—looking at words and identifying them, without guessing. With higher-interest stories, the reader becomes preoccupied with the content of the story and reverts to habitual, inappropriate decoding strategies, which means that errors increase greatly. Later in the program, after students have practiced the game of accurate decoding, the stories become more interesting. Although the content "distracts" the reader, appropriate strategies are now strong enough for the reader to read with acceptable accuracy.

During Lessons 1 through 10, students read only isolated sentences (totaling about 75–100 words). The stories begin in Lesson 11 and continue in each lesson. Their length increases from about 200 words to 600 words by Lesson 65.

Students receive practice in comprehension skills with the following activities:

◆ Orally answering questions about each part of the story after reading the part within an error limit

◆ Writing answers to a variety of comprehension items that require recall of story events, sequencing, and characters

The daily Individual Reading Checkouts provide each student with a lot of practice in reading connected sentences. Because the students work in pairs, the entire checkout doesn't take very long—about 10 minutes for both checkouts. The daily timed reading checkouts help students gradually develop acceptable reading rates (from 55 words per minute at the beginning of Level B1 to 90 words per minute at the end of Level B1).

The Workbook Exercises are carefully integrated with the Word-Attack Activities and with the stories that the students read. From lesson to lesson, there is a careful development of skills in the Workbook.

> **IT IS VERY IMPORTANT
> FOR THE STUDENTS TO DO THE WORKBOOK
> EXERCISES AS PART OF EACH LESSON.**

Each Workbook lesson is one page. The different activities provide students with practice in writing sounds, copying, answering comprehension questions, spelling, and transforming words. Many of the activities deal with word details because these are the details the problem reader tends to ignore.

Outcome Behavior

Upon completion of **Decoding B1,** students' progress can be seen in both improved accuracy and improved rate. Following is one part of the story from Lesson 65. Students can read this passage with 98 percent accuracy and at a minimum rate of 90 words per minute.

> Jean was trying to think of everything that had happened just before the drams went to sleep. She remembered how she had been running with the drams biting her. She ran and fell into a hole in the floor. She remembered getting out of the hole and running again.
>
> But were the drams biting her then? "Think, think."
>
> "No," Jean said to herself. "I don't remember being bitten after I fell into the hole. Something must have happened before I fell into the hole." Jean tried to think of everything that happened before she fell into the hole. She looked at the beach. More drams were marching closer to the barracks. They were marching over the sleeping drams. "Bzzzzzzzzzzz."

▶ Changes in the 1999 Edition of Decoding B1

The 1999 edition of **Decoding B1**

◆ has a number of design changes and changes that update the material students read. The major change, however, has to do with the redesign of the early lessons in the program. The revision focused on the problems experienced by students who passed the placement test criteria to enter **Decoding B1** but did not go through the **Decoding A** program. A fair percentage of the students were able to read whole words but had no understanding of the relationship between letters and the sounds they usually make. These students floundered in the early lessons of **Decoding B1.** Through their teacher's persistence and the tasks that required that students respond to letter sounds, these students finally acquired understanding of letter-sound relationships.

◆ The 1999 edition of **Decoding B1** has beginning lessons that are far less laborious in teaching letter-sound relationships these students haven't learned. The first ten lessons of the program provide a strong focus on sounds in isolation and identifying the sounds that specific letters make in words. Students also read sentences that contain word types they are learning. By Lesson 11, they have a sufficiently solid basis in letter-sound relationships to learn sound combinations and to read stories composed of the words they have studied.

▶ Decoding B2 Decoding Strategies

▪ Who It's For

Decoding B2 is appropriate for students in grades 3 through 12 who have some decoding problems, who do not read at an adequate rate, who still tend to confuse words with similar spellings, and who tend to make word-guessing mistakes.

▪ What Is Taught

Decoding B2 follows the same format as Decoding B1. Each lessson is divided into four major parts:

1 Word-Attack Skills

2 Group Reading

3 Individual Reading Checkouts

4 Workbook Exercises

The following activities are included in **Word-Attack Skills.**

◆ Identifying the sounds of letter combinations **(tch, ir, ur, er, wa, oi, ce, ci, tion, ea, ge, gi, kn)** and reading words with those combinations

◆ Reading lists of regularly spelled words, such as **risks,** and irregularly spelled words, such as **league**

◆ Reading words that contain difficult consonant blends **(flip, drop, splash)**

◆ Reading words with endings **(dropping, rested)**

◆ Reading silent-**e** words **(fine, taped)**

◆ Reading compound words **(greenhouse)**

◆ Practicing pattern drills that demonstrate consistent phonic relationships **(sigh, sight, night, fight, flight)**

The stories in **Decoding B2** increase in length, difficulty, and interest. All stories are composed of words that have been taught in **Decoding B2** or words that the students can already read. The syntax and structure of the stories are designed for the problem decoder and are designed to correct the mistakes the reader typically makes. Story length increases from about 500 words to nearly 900 words by Lesson 65.

Students receive practice in comprehension skills by orally answering questions about each part of the story after reading the part within an error limit and writing answers to a variety of comprehension items that require recall of story events, sequencing, and characters.

The daily Individual Reading Checkouts help students develop both accuracy and reading rates (from 90 words per minute at the beginning of Level B2 to 120 words per minute at the end of Level B2).

The Workbook Exercises are carefully integrated with the Word-Attack Activities and with the stories that the students read.

> ## IT IS VERY IMPORTANT
> ## FOR THE STUDENTS TO DO THE WORKBOOK
> ## EXERCISES AS PART OF EACH LESSON.

Outcome Behavior

Upon completion of **Decoding B2,** students' progress can be seen in both improved accuracy and improved rate. Following is one part of the story from Lesson 53. Students can read this passage with 98 percent accuracy and at a minimum rate of 115 words per minute.

Tony's hands were sore. His back was sore. So were his legs. He was beginning to realize that Salt had been right when he'd said that the real work was just beginning. For the past three hours, Tony had hauled rocks from the pile. At first the pile had been about two meters high. Now it was only about half a meter high.

Tony bent down and grabbed another rock. When he picked it up, he saw something below it. "Hey, Rosa," he said. "What's that?"

Rosa tossed a rock into the underbrush. Then she wiped the sweat from her eyes. She bent down and looked where Tony was pointing. "It looks like a knife handle," Rosa said. "I'll pull it out."

▶ *Changes in the 1999 Edition of Decoding B2*

The 1999 edition of **Decoding B2**

◆ has a number of design changes and changes that update the material students read. The major change, however, has to do with the redesign of the early lessons in the program. The revision focused on the problems experienced by students who passed the placement test criteria to enter **Decoding B2** but did not know all of the sound combinations (such as **ir, ou, ar, ea, igh, oul**) that are taught in the **Decoding B1** program. These students frequently made many word-reading errors, particularly on words that contain sound combinations, in the early lessons of **Decoding B2**. Sound-combination review exercises are provided in Lessons 1, 2, and 3 of the 1999 edition of **Decoding B2**.

◆ Another skill that was difficult for students who started **Decoding B2** but had not gone through the **Decoding B1** program was rewriting words that have endings **(striped, jogged)** without those endings **(stripe, jog)**. Additional prompts were added to the early lessons in **Decoding B2** to better teach this skill.

◆ Finally, some stories that begin in **Decoding B1** continue in **Decoding B2**. A story introduction is provided in this revised edition.

With these changes in the 1999 edition of **Decoding B2**, students who qualify for the program are able to proceed in it successfully.

▶ Decoding C Skill Applications

Who It's For

Students who complete **Decoding B2** demonstrate considerable improvement in reading accuracy and rate, but in that program, they are not confronted with either the vocabulary or the sentence forms that appear in textbooks. The passive voice, the use of parenthetical (nonrestrictive) clauses, the longer multiclause sentences, and similar constructions are deliberately avoided in **Decoding B1** and **B2. Decoding C** is appropriate for fair readers in grades 4 through 12 who have mastered many basic reading skills but who have trouble with multisyllabic words and typical textbook material.

What Is Taught

Decoding C emphasizes Word-Attack Skills, accurate story reading, informational reading, comprehension questions, Individual Reading Checkouts, and Workbook applications.

The following activities are included in **Word-Attack Skills.**

◆ A review of words containing letter combinations such as **th, oa, ea, ai, ou, ar, ir, er, ur, igh, oi, tion, ce, ci, ge, gi**

◆ Introduction of the sounds for the letter combinations **ure, aw, au, tial, cial**

◆ Introduction of the meaning of more than 500 vocabulary words

◆ Introduction of the affixes **ex, ly, un, re, dis, pre, tri, sub, less, ness, able**

◆ Practice in reading words containing various letter combinations and affixes

◆ Practice in writing complex words as root words plus affixes

The following activities provide practice in **Selection Reading Skills.**

◆ Reading selections that give specific factual information on a particular topic

◆ Reading selections that are fictional

◆ Reading selections that contain a high percentage of new words

◆ Reading selections from magazines, newspapers, and other sources

The following activities provide practice in reading **comprehension skills.**

◆ Orally answering questions about the selections that are read

◆ Writing answers to a variety of comprehension items, including both literal and inferential items that require recall of story events, sequencing, and characters

Goal

One goal of **Decoding C** is to maintain and consolidate the skills that were taught in **Decoding B1** and **B2. Decoding C** is designed to provide continued practice on skills taught earlier so that the correct application of the skills becomes habitual.

Goal

Another goal is to provide a transition between tightly controlled syntax and vocabulary presentations, such as those in **Decoding B1** and **B2,** and presentations typically encountered in traditional reading materials. The presentation of new reading vocabulary is simplified in **Decoding C.** Little prompting is provided; most new words are introduced by a simple test statement: **What word?** In **Decoding B1** and **B2,** new words are taught in the Word-Attack Exercises for several lessons before they appear in stories. In **Decoding C,** new words may appear only once in Word-Attack Exercises before being included in the stories. The purpose of this accelerated strategy is to develop students' ability to learn new words quickly.

To bridge the gap between students' performance level at the end of **Decoding B2** and the level required to read textbooks and other informational material, **Decoding C** introduces several sentence types and conventions that characterize text material. Qualifiers such as *nevertheless, indeed,* and *frequently* receive considerable use in **Decoding C.** The use of passive voice, nonrestrictive clauses, sentences that define words, and other mechanical features of nonfictional discourse are also introduced.

Goal

Another goal is to present the meaning of words frequently encountered in text materials. Vocabulary words are presented so that students are introduced to the meanings of new words before reading those words in selections. Many of the more than 500 words included in the vocabulary exercises are words the students have already encountered; however, students frequently have only a vague, peripheral, or incorrect notion of their meaning.

Goal

Another goal is to help students apply the decoding skills taught in the program to reading material encountered outside the program, such as Student Books, newspapers, and magazines. In the second half of the program, students apply the same skills they used with in-program passages to selections taken from outside reading material. The selections deal with topics of interest to the students. **Decoding C** demonstrates to students that they have the ability to apply their decoding skills to a wide variety of reading matter, and that they are capable of decoding such material successfully.

Outcome Behavior

Students who complete **Decoding C** are fluent decoders who make only occasional decoding errors when they read materials that contain a fairly broad vocabulary and a variety of sentence forms. They can read the following passage with better than 99 percent accuracy and at a minimum rate of about 150 words per minute.

GALEN'S THEORIES

Around 1500, some doctors began to question the medical theories that had been accepted for hundreds of years. These doctors exhibited a great deal of courage because most people were suspicious of anybody who challenged established theories.

But a few doctors had the courage to record what they observed even though their observations were in conflict with long-standing theories and with the accepted medical practice of the time. The basic theory of medicine around 1500 had been accepted for over a thousand years. It had been developed by a man named Galen, a Greek who tried to explain how the body worked and how to cure its ailments.[1]

During Galen's time, doctors were not permitted to dissect (cut up) dead bodies. Galen realized, however, that doctors could not work with the human body unless they understood the anatomy of the body. (The study of anatomy deals with the structure of the body–the bones, muscles, nerves, and organs.) Galen wrote an elaborate work on anatomy. He drew conclusions about human anatomy by studying the anatomy of different animals. Since he couldn't work on human bodies, he dissected animals, such as pigs and apes.[2]

Galen proclaimed that human hipbones looked like those of an ox—a conclusion based upon his dissection of oxen. Galen thought that different human organs were identical to those found in the hog, the dog, the ox, or the ape. He made these mistakes because his conclusions about human anatomy were based upon animal anatomy instead of human anatomy.

Students who complete **Decoding C** are capable of reading with enough accuracy so that their comprehension will no longer be distorted by misreading the words. They are able to decode at a rate sufficient to facilitate comprehension of what they read.

The students can demonstrate accuracy and rate capabilities across a range of syntax, vocabulary, format, and content. They have the ability to learn new information rapidly and well enough to apply it after one reading of an informational selection.

Although students may have comprehension deficits that affect their overall reading performance, their decoding problems may be considered remedied when they successfully complete **Decoding C.**

The Comprehension Programs

Below is a diagram of the four Comprehension programs in SRA's *Corrective Reading* series.

1 Comprehension A
5 preprogram lessons
60 regular lessons
7 Fact Game lessons

2 Comprehension B1
60 regular lessons
12 Fact Game/Mastery Test lessons

3 Comprehension B2
65 regular lessons
7 Fact Game/Mastery Test lessons

4 Comprehension C
140 regular lessons
9 Fact Game/Mastery Test lessons

Introduction to the 1999 Edition

The 1999 edition of the Comprehension programs has a number of changes designed to make the teacher material easier for teachers to use and the student materials more attractive for students. Some program content changes addressed problematic items in the 1988 edition of the student materials.

The Comprehension Programs and the Poor Comprehender

The Comprehension programs are designed to change the behavior of the poor comprehender. The specific tendencies of this student suggest what a program must do to be effective in changing the student's behavior.

Because students who are low in comprehension skills are often poor decoders, they typically do not follow instructions precisely. They have often been reinforced for raising their hand and asking the teacher questions. This strategy has served them in content areas, such as science and social studies, as well as "reading." As a result, they have not developed precision in following instructions that are presented orally or in writing.

Because of the way material they have studied has been sequenced, **poor comprehenders also have a poor memory for information.** Typically, they have never been required to learn information one day and then use it that day and from then on. The usual pattern has been for them to work with vocabulary or facts for only a lesson or two, after which the material disappears. The result is a very poorly developed strategy for remembering information, particularly systems of information that contain related facts and rules.

Poor comprehenders also have poor statement-repetition skills

(primarily because they have never practiced these skills). For instance, if told to repeat the statement "Some of the people who live in America are illiterate," the students may say, "Some people who live in America are ill," or some other inaccurate production. The lack of statement-repetition skills places these students at a great disadvantage when they try to read and retain information, even if they decode it correctly.

Poor comprehenders lack the analytical skills required to process arguments. Often they vascillate from being very guarded in

believing what others tell them, to being very gullible. They often have very strong feelings and prejudices, but they are unable to articulate the evidence that supports their beliefs or the conclusions that derive from the evidence. They are not practiced with flaws in arguments that present false analogies, improper deductions, or appeals that are inappropriate (such as arguing about a whole group from information about an individual).

Poor comprehenders have a deficiency in vocabulary and common information. This deficiency prevents them from constructing the

appropriate schemata when reading about situations that assume basic information or vocabulary. They may understand the meaning of the word *colonial*, for instance, but not know the relationship of that word to *colony*.

Finally, poor comprehenders are not highly motivated students.

For these students, reading had been punishing. The students often profess indifference: "I don't care if I learn that or not." But the students' behavior gives strong suggestions that they care a great deal. When they learn to use new words such as *regulate* and *participate*, they feel very proud.

The students' ineffective reading strategies and negative attitudes about reading become more ingrained as the readers get older. To overcome them requires a very careful program, one that systematically replaces the strategies with new ones and that provides lots and lots of practice.

In summary, the knowledge and skills of poor comprehenders are spotty. While often exhibiting intelligent behaviors in dealing with their peers, they are remarkably naive in dealing with academic content because they don't know exactly what to attend to, precisely what it means, how to organize it, how to relate it to other known facts and remember it, how to apply it to unique situations, and how to evaluate it in terms of consistency with other facts and rules.

The Solutions

SRA's *Corrective Reading* Comprehension programs provide these solutions to the problems of the poor comprehender.

The Comprehension programs are designed to provide extensive practice in following directions.
The various activities presented in the programs are designed so that students must attend to the instructions. In one lesson, for instance, the directions for an activity may be "Circle the verbs." In the next lesson, instructions for the same activity may be "Make a box around the verbs." The direct-instruction activities that address following instructions present directions that the students cannot figure out from either the format of the activity or the context. Students, therefore, learn the strategy of reading carefully and attending to the **details** of the instructions. Also, students practice writing instructions so they develop an appreciation of what information is needed to clearly convey the operation.

The Comprehension programs provide daily practice in statement repetition in Levels A, B1, and B2.
This practice is presented in Level A through tasks that don't involve reading. In later levels, the statement-repetition activities are related increasingly to statements the students read. The emphasis on statement repetition both makes students much more facile in repeating statements (requiring only one or two attempts, compared to the many attempts that would be required early in the program) and helps reinforce the general strategy that one must be very precise when dealing with statements in what is read as well as in what is heard.

The Comprehension programs are designed so that whatever is taught is used.
In the programs, nothing goes away. The vocabulary that is introduced is integrated so the students use the vocabulary in following instructions, making analogies and deductions, identifying flaws in arguments, and in various other activities. Similarly, facts that are learned are integrated and applied to a wide range of applications. This nonspiral approach to instruction demonstrates to students that they must develop strategies for retaining the information that is taught and relating it to other information. The format assures that students will learn how to learn, organize, and process what is taught. Fact Games and Mastery Tests within the programs document to both teacher and students that the skills and information presented in the program are mastered.

The programs present various analytical skills that can be applied to higher-order thinking tasks. In fact, the *Corrective Reading* Comprehension programs are possibly the only readily available source of instruction for teaching students how analogies work, how logical reasoning is applied to arguments, how conclusions depend on evidence, and how to evaluate the adequacy of the evidence. Deductions are emphasized, because basic arguments that affect everyday life are usually presented as deductions. The programs present specific common fallacies (arguing from part to whole, arguing from whole to part, arguing from a false cause, arguing from limited choices). Students also learn to identify contradictions, at first simple ones, and later, those that are inferred from facts the students have learned. The focus of the programs, in other words, is not simply on narrowly defined logical-reasoning skills, but on logical-reasoning skills as they apply to all aspects of reading.

To compensate for the deficiencies in vocabulary and common information, the programs introduce both "fact systems" and vocabulary words. The fact systems that have been selected include: body systems (skeletal, muscular, circulatory, etc.), calendar information, animal information (classifications such as fish, amphibian, reptile, mammal, bird), economic rules (supply-demand), and plants. These systems provide a vehicle for teaching some vocabulary. Additional vocabulary is introduced in all levels. In Levels B1 and B2, vocabulary is introduced in connection with parts of speech. Some of these words were selected because they have a verb, noun, and adjective form (for example, *protect*, *protection*, and *protective*). In Level C, students are taught how to infer the meaning of words from context. Note that all words, once introduced, appear in various activities—from following instructions to identifying contradictions.

Finally, the programs address the problem of the poor comprehender's low self-image. The programs are designed so the students can succeed in learning sophisticated skills (such as identifying the missing premise in an argument). Furthermore, a point system that is based on realistic performance goals assures that the student who tries will succeed and will receive reinforcement for improved performance.

In summary, the programs use a two-pronged approach. Each level teaches specific skills to replace the student's ineffective approach to comprehension. Each level also contains an effective management system that turns students on to reading. The approach **works.**

Progress Through the Comprehension Programs

The programs are designed so that there is a careful progression of skill development from level to level.

There are **THREE** entry points.

1 Students who begin at

Level A

should complete A and B1 in a school year
(a total of 125 lessons)

2 Students who begin at

Level B1

should complete B1 and B2 in a school year
(a total of 125 lessons)

3 Students who begin at

Level C

should complete C and additional
outside reading in a school year

A summary of the programs follows. For each program, the summary describes (a) the reading behavior of students typically placed in that program, (b) what is taught, and (c) what students should be able to do at the end of the program.

Comprehension A Thinking Basics

Who It's For

Comprehension A is designed for poor comprehenders in grades 3 through 12 who speak and understand basic English and whose scores on the *Corrective Reading* Comprehension Placement Test indicate that they belong in the program. These students may have been identified as educable mentally retarded (EMR), learning disabled, educationally handicapped, or perceptually handicapped. The program is not appropriate for students who speak no English, or whose grasp of English is quite weak.

Tryouts of **Comprehension A** with average students in grades 1 through 3 demonstrated that the program provides solid reinforcement in comprehension skills for whatever reading system is being taught.

Students who place in **Comprehension A** do not understand the concepts underlying much of the material being taught in classrooms. They do not have well-developed recitation skills. They cannot repeat sentences they hear, so they have trouble retaining and answering questions about information that is presented. These students are often prevented from comprehending what they read because they don't even understand the material when it is presented orally.

What Is Taught

The skills taught in **Comprehension A** fall into three broad categories: Thinking Operations, Workbook Exercises, and Information.

Thinking Operations concentrate on those general operations useful to students in solving a wide range of problems. These operations apply to virtually any content area. Here are the specific skill areas (tracks) taught in Thinking Operations.

- ▲ Analogies
- ▲ And/Or
- ▲ Basic Evidence
- ▲ Classification
- ▲ Deductions
- ▲ Definitions
- ▲ Description
- ▲ Inductions
- ▲ Opposites
- ▲ Same
- ▲ Statement Inference
- ▲ True-False

Workbook Exercises provide students with practice in applying the skills taught in Thinking Operations and the facts taught in Information. Workbook practice serves as a bridge between teacher-directed activities and those in which the student uses the skills independently. Here are the skills practiced in the Workbooks.

▲ Analogies

▲ Classification

▲ Deductions

▲ Description

▲ Inductions

▲ Same

▲ True-False

Information Exercises are designed (1) to teach information that should be useful to students, and (2) to give students practice in organizing groups of related facts. Probably more important than the actual information taught is the practice students get in learning groups of related facts. Facility in learning new names comes with practice, and any body of related information will help to meet the need for practice. Of course, it is best if the information is also useful. Here are the tracks taught in Information.

▲ Calendar (months, seasons, holidays)

▲ Poems

▲ Animals (mammals, reptiles, etc.; felines, canines; herbivorous, carnivorous)

Outcome Behavior

At the end of **Comprehension A,** students are able to handle items such as the following.

═══════ EXERCISE 7 ═══════

ANALOGIES: Synonyms

Here's an analogy about words.
Ask is to **inquire** as **weep** is to. . . . (Pause 2 seconds.) Get ready. (Signal.) *Cry.*

Everybody, say that analogy. (Signal.) *Ask is to inquire as weep is to cry.*

Lesson 59, Exercise 7 from Comprehension A TPB A2

═══════ EXERCISE 10 ═══════

DEFINITIONS

Listen. The buffalo ambled to the pond. Say that. (Signal.) *The buffalo ambled to the pond.* (Repeat until firm.)

Now say that sentence with different words for **ambled.** (Pause.)
Get ready. (Signal.) *The buffalo walked slowly to the pond.* (Repeat until firm.)

Lesson 59, Exercise 10 from Comprehension A TPB A2

B

1. lizard, bat, trunk	(objects)	actions	tell what kind
2. sprinkle, swim, shoot	objects	(actions)	tell what kind
3. healthy, slick, dry	objects	actions	(tell what kind)
4. exhibit, bush, tiger	(objects)	actions	tell what kind
5. deduce, decrease, dig	objects	(actions)	tell what kind

Lesson 59, Part B from Comprehension A Workbook

BASIC EVIDENCE: Using Facts

The next Thinking Operation is **Basic Evidence.**

1. You're going to use two facts to explain things that happened. (Hold up one finger.) First fact. Louis owned an expensive diamond. Say it. (Signal.) *Louis owned an expensive diamond.* (Repeat until firm.) (Hold up two fingers.) Second fact. The diamond was very well hidden. Say it. (Signal.) *The diamond was very well hidden.* (Repeat until firm.)

2. Everybody, say those facts again. (Hold up one finger.) First fact. *Louis owned an expensive diamond.* (Hold up two fingers.) Second fact. *The diamond was very well hidden.* (Repeat until the students say the facts in order.)

> ***Individual test***
> Call on individual students to say the facts.

3. Here's what happened. He didn't bother to get a burglar alarm. Tell me the fact that explains **why** that happened. (Pause.) Get ready. (Signal.) *The diamond was very well hidden.*

4. Listen. First fact. Louis owned an expensive diamond. Second fact. The diamond was very well hidden.

5. Here's what happened. He bought insurance. Tell me the fact that explains **why** that happened. (Pause.) Get ready. (Signal.) *Louis owned an expensive diamond.*

6. Here's what happened. Some robbers broke into his apartment. Tell me the fact that explains **why** that happened. (Pause.) Get ready. (Signal.) *Louis owned an expensive diamond.*

7. Here's what happened. The robbers were still looking for the diamond when the police showed up. Tell me the fact that explains **why** that happened. (Pause.) Get ready. (Signal.) *The diamond was very well hidden.*

8. (Repeat steps 5–7 until firm.)

Lesson 59, Exercise 13 from Comprehension A TPB A2

The students are able to recite poems, give functional definitions for approximately 50 words, including **indolent, herbivorous,** and **majority,** and perform a variety of tasks in following instructions. Although students will still have an enormous number of comprehension skills to learn, they now have a foundation on which to build.

Comprehension B1 and B2
Comprehension Skills

Who They're For

Comprehension B1 and **B2** are designed for poor comprehenders in grades 4 through 12 who understand English. **Comprehension B1** is appropriate for students whose scores on the *Corrective Reading* Comprehension Placement Test indicate that they belong in the program. **Comprehension B2** is appropriate for students who have completed **Comprehension B1. Comprehension B2** is not an entry point for the Comprehension series.

The programs are appropriate for students who may have been identified as educable mentally retarded (EMR), learning disabled, educationally handicapped, or perceptually handicapped. The programs are not appropriate for students who speak no English, or whose grasp of English is quite weak.

Tryouts of **Comprehension B1** and **B2** with average students in grades 2 through 4 demonstrated that the programs provide solid reinforcement in comprehension skills for whatever reading system is being taught.

Students who place in **Comprehension B1** exhibit many of the deficiencies observed in students who place in **Comprehension A.** They lack some common basic information, such as how many months are in a year. They are deficient in thinking operations, but usually they are more advanced in thinking operations than Level A students are. They tend to have trouble with difficult statement-repetition tasks, deductions that involve *maybe,* relating conclusions to evidence, identifying contradictions, following written directions, and writing. Their deficiencies in vocabulary and information make it difficult for them to perform many reading comprehension activities.

What Is Taught

Reading comprehension is a complex process that requires a number of separate skills. For example, when students are asked to write answers to questions about a written passage, they may have to use the following skills.

▲ Formulate a deduction (reasoning skill)

▲ Understand basic classes (information skill)

▲ Identify the precise meaning of a word (vocabulary skill)

▲ Understand the structure of complicated sentences (sentence skill)

▲ Answer a question or follow a direction (basic comprehension skill)

▲ Write their answers correctly (writing skill)

Students who have mastered these skills are more likely to understand what they read. Therefore, **Comprehension B1** and **B2** teach all these skills, many of which are developed from skills taught earlier. The teaching is done so that what is introduced is used, applied, reinforced, and repeated with sufficient frequency to assure mastery.

The skills that are taught can be grouped into several skill areas.

▲ Reasoning skills

▲ Information skills

▲ Vocabulary skills

▲ Sentence skills

▲ Comprehension skills

▲ Writing skills

Reasoning Skills. Textbook material that students are expected to read usually proceeds on an implicitly logical basis. Students who don't grasp the logic underlying a passage probably won't be able to answer questions about the passage that involve any sort of analogy, deduction, or rule application. They will experience difficulty when they try to defend an interpretation of the passage or identify contradictory elements in the passage.

The following tracks teach reasoning skills: Deductions, Basic Evidence, Analogies, Contradictions, and Similes.

■ The Deductions track introduces basic reasoning strategies. The students learn how to draw conclusions and how to apply rules to diverse situations.

■ The Basic Evidence track teaches the students to distinguish between what does and what does not follow from a given fact or rule.

■ The Analogies track introduces another basic reasoning strategy. The students learn how to formulate analogies and how to understand what analogies imply.

■ The Contradictions track teaches the students to recognize contradictions and shows them how to analyze flaws in passages.

■ The Similes track teaches the students to understand figurative language and the relationships implied by such language. Students learn to analyze and to create similes.

Information Skills. Students who do not have an adequate store of common information are at a disadvantage when they read selections that assume possession of such common information. Typically, such students will not know basic classifications, the names of such things as body systems and body organs, or basic rules about how things work. Moreover, they frequently lack a systematic method of retaining new information because they are unpracticed in organizing groups of related facts.

The following tracks teach information skills: Classification, Body Systems, Body Rules, and Economics Rules.

- The Classification track teaches the students various conventional categories and rules for determining how to put objects into categories.
- The Body Systems track teaches the names and parts of the major body systems. The track also provides the students with a successful experience in mastering a group of related facts.
- The Body Rules track teaches rules that explain how the various body systems work. The students use the skills taught in the Deductions track to apply those rules.
- The Economics Rules track introduces rules that help the students become more knowledgeable consumers. The track also extends the students' experience in applying rules to diverse situations.

Vocabulary Skills. Students with a limited vocabulary encounter many unfamiliar words when they read material designed for their grade level. They may not know how to look up words in a dictionary or how to interpret a definition if they find it. They also may not understand such things as how different affixes affect the meaning of a word.

All vocabulary skills are taught in the Definitions track. This track teaches many new words and general procedures that help the students understand new words. All words taught in the Definitions track are carefully integrated into other tracks in the program.

Sentence Skills. Students with a faulty understanding of basic sentence structure will have difficulty comprehending complicated Student Book sentences. Those students may be unfamiliar with the classification of sentence parts. Because of their lack of understanding of sentence structure, it is often difficult to discuss written materials with them.

The following tracks teach sentence skills: Parts of Speech, Subject/Predicate, Sentence Combinations, and Sentence Analysis.

- The Parts of Speech track teaches the students to identify nouns, verbs, and adjectives in sentences. The students learn to look at sentences in terms of their structure.
- The Subject/Predicate track teaches the students to identify subjects and predicates. They also learn that parts of certain predicates can be placed in front of the subject.
- The Sentence Combinations track teaches the students how to combine sentences by using such words as *however* and *especially.* The students also learn how those words relate one sentence part to another.
- The Sentence Analysis track gives the students practice in breaking down complex sentences into their simple-sentence components. After the students have mastered sentence-combination techniques, they are given complex sentences to rewrite in simple-sentence form.

Basic Comprehension Skills. Students who have difficulty answering questions or following directions seldom are able to show that they comprehend what they read, even though their comprehension might be adequate.

The following tracks teach two basic comprehension skills: Statement Inference and Following Directions.

■ The Statement Inference track teaches the students to answer questions based on simple sentences at first and, later, on extended passages. Often, the students are required to explain how they arrived at the answer to a particular question. The sentences and passages the students read incorporate the vocabulary, rules, and information presented in other tracks. Many passages elaborate upon the Body Systems and Economics Rules tracks.

■ The Following Directions track teaches the students to draw a picture by following a set of directions. The directions emphasize the function of prepositions and also make extensive use of vocabulary, rules, and information.

Writing Skills. Students who do not have adequate writing skills are likely to be misunderstood. They tend to make errors in punctuation and grammar, and they also tend to repeat themselves. They are particularly weak in the use of descriptive prose.

The following tracks teach writing skills: Writing Directions, Writing Paragraphs, Editing, and Writing Stories.

■ The Writing Directions track is the reverse of the Following Directions track. In Following Directions, students follow written directions to draw a picture. In Writing Directions, students are given a picture and then write a set of directions for creating that picture.

■ The Writing Paragraphs track requires students to rewrite carefully controlled paragraphs by combining sentences and correcting mistakes. The track helps students to become more facile with the paragraph form and more practiced in the writing of extended passages.

■ The Editing track teaches the students to correct many different kinds of writing mistakes, such as redundancy, faulty subject-verb agreement, and incorrect punctuation.

■ The Writing Stories track allows the students to apply their newly acquired writing skills in a creative manner. After the students finish their daily Workbook exercises, they are to write a story about a picture that appears in the back of the Workbook. The stories provide the teacher with tangible evidence of the students' writing ability.

After a new skill is taught in a particular track, that skill is applied in many other tracks. For example, the word **artery** is introduced in the Body Systems track. It is then used in Analogies, Deductions, Writing, Following Directions, Sentence Combinations, and Body Rules.

The overall sequencing in **Comprehension B1** and **B2** places increasing demands on writing performance as students progress through the program.

Outcome Behavior

After completing **Comprehension B2,** students have learned many of the skills associated with reading carefully, operating on information that they read, and following specific instructions. Although students may lack specific information—particularly information about vocabulary—they have the important skills necessary to perform reading-comprehension exercises. For example, they may not know the definition of all words, but they can decode a statement with a definition, determining which word is being defined and which words define it. They also understand the definitions of some words and are able to place those words in sentences. The exercise to the right shows some of the definitions that students in **Comprehension B1** and **B2** have learned.

G Fill in each blank with the word that has the same meaning as the word or words under the blank.

1. We stayed until the ____conclusion____ of
(end)
the concert.

2. Dentists ____examine____ many teeth
(look at)
every day.

3. Some things are very easy to
____criticize____.
(find fault with)

4. People cannot ____produce____ storms.
(make)

5. To save gas, this car must be ____modified____.
(changed)

Lesson 28, part G from Comprehension B2 Workbook

E Draw in the arrows. Tell if each tube is a vein or an artery. Tell what gas each tube carries.

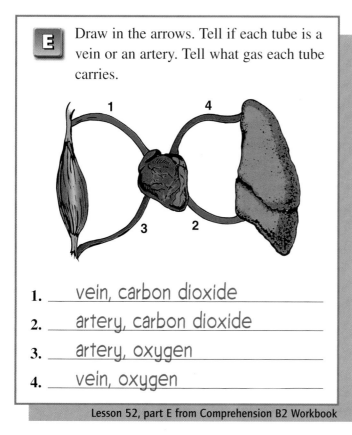

1. ____vein, carbon dioxide____
2. ____artery, carbon dioxide____
3. ____artery, oxygen____
4. ____vein, oxygen____

Lesson 52, part E from Comprehension B2 Workbook

Students who finish **Comprehension B2** don't know the details of every system (such as solar systems, plant classification systems, etc.), but they do understand what systems are and how they work. They know that a system is made up of parts that have names and that a system is governed by rules. They can handle systems-related information and can complete exercises like the one to the left. The exercise is from **Comprehension B2,** Lesson 52.

1 Write a word that comes from **acquire** or **participate** in each blank. Then write **verb**, **noun**, or **adjective** after each item.

1. Soccer is a ___participatory___ sport.
   ___adjective___

2. Mary was selected to ___participate___ in the school play. ___verb___

3. Some people choose to limit their ___participation___ in sports. ___noun___

4. Jim can't afford to ___acquire___ any more shoes. ___verb___

5. A car is an expensive ___acquisition___.
   ___noun___

Lesson 63, part I from Comprehension B2 Workbook

The students do not know all parts of speech when they complete the program; however, they understand that when words function in the same way, they are the same part of speech. For example, a word representing the action in a sentence will always be the verb. Students also understand that the construction of a word often indicates its part of speech. For example, the endings of words like **selective**, **consumable**, and **explanatory** indicate that the words are adjectives. The students show their ability to work with parts of speech in exercises like the one shown at left, which is from **Comprehension B2**, Lesson 63.

Upon completing the program, students do not understand every type of fallacy contained within faulty arguments, but they do understand the basic procedures for drawing conclusions from facts, which is the first step in recognizing faulty arguments. In exercises like the one that follows, students develop the ability to draw conclusions from facts. The exercise is from **Comprehension B1**, Lesson 46.

1 Write the conclusion of each deduction.

1. Muscles do not move the bones they cover. A gastrocnemius is a muscle.
   ___So, a gastrocnemius does not move the bone it covers.___

2. Some people who eat a lot get fat. Harry is a person who eats a lot.
   ___So, maybe Harry will get fat.___

3. Every fish can swim. A snake is not a fish.
   ___So, nothing.___

Lesson 46, part I from Comprehension B1 Workbook

Another step in understanding faulty arguments is to determine which evidence in the argument is relevant to the argument and which evidence is irrelevant. At the end of **Comprehension B2**, students have developed this skill and can do tasks like the one below. The task is from **Comprehension B2**, Lesson 4.

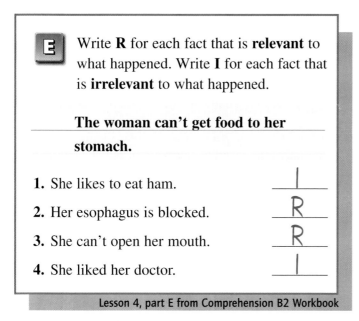

E Write **R** for each fact that is **relevant** to what happened. Write **I** for each fact that is **irrelevant** to what happened.

The woman can't get food to her stomach.

1. She likes to eat ham.   I
2. Her esophagus is blocked.   R
3. She can't open her mouth.   R
4. She liked her doctor.   I

Lesson 4, part E from Comprehension B2 Workbook

The first step in critiquing an argument is to determine whether it is internally consistent. In order to determine internal consistency, one must be able to identify possible inconsistencies. **Comprehension B1** and **B2** teach students how to do this. By the end of **Comprehension B2**, students can handle exercises like the one shown below. The exercise is from **Comprehension B2**, Lesson 31.

G Underline the contradiction. Circle the statement it contradicts. Tell **why** the underlined statement contradicts the circled statement.

From the outside, your upper arm looks pretty simple. But inside, many complex things are happening. Arteries are carrying blood to your biceps. Sense nerves are sending feelings to the brain. * The nerves carry little bits of electricity. The arteries carry carbon dioxide. All this is going on, but you never have to think about it.

Because arteries carry oxygen to the biceps

Lesson 31, part G from Comprehension B2 Workbook

At the end of **Comprehension B2,** students can follow very specific instructions of the sort found in work applications, tax returns, and other similar forms. The following exercise, from Lesson 44 of **Comprehension B2,** is an example of what they can do.

J Use the facts to fill out the form.

> **Facts: Your name is Brian Ozaki. You have just graduated from State University in Rushville, with a B.A. degree in journalism. You are applying for a job with a newspaper. You were editor of your high school and college newspapers. You are twenty-two years old. You are single and unemployed. Your address is 22 W. Main, Farmington, NM. You want to write for the sports page.**

Instructions:

1. Name, last name first (please print):
   Ozaki, Brian

2. Colleges or universities attended:
   State University in Rushville

3. Degrees, if any:
   B.A.

4. Journalism experience, if any:
   Editor of high school and college newspapers

5. Current employer:
   (None)

6. Are you married? ____ No

7. Address: ____ 22 W. Main
   Farmington, NM

8. What section do you prefer to write for?
   Sports

Lesson 44, part J from Comprehension B2 Workbook

Students who have completed **Comprehension B2** do not know all the rules of correct writing; however, they have had practice in reading material while attending to its form. They have edited material to eliminate incorrect grammar, redundancies, and punctuation errors. Performance on passages like the one below demonstrates their basic understanding of writing form. The passage is from **Comprehension B2**, Lesson 65.

 Underline the redundant sentences.
Circle and correct the punctuation errors.
Cross out and correct the wording errors.

Duke Ellington was the greatest jazz band leader ~~what~~ that ever lived. He formed his first band in the 1920s,which was when jazz first became popular. Although many of the players changed,the band stayed together for almost fifty ~~year~~ years. No band leader was better than Ellington. Everybody wanted to play with Ellington; consequently,he had no trouble finding the best players. The Ellington band could really swing.All kinds of players wanted to belong to it.

Lesson 65, part G from Comprehension B2 Workbook

Comprehension B1 and **B2** teach basic skills that set the stage for more sophisticated skill applications. The students are provided with the basic skills needed to understand what is read and to understand some of the conventions associated with the written word. With these basic abilities, they can readily learn how to identify fallacies in arguments, how to read critically, and how to resolve possible inconsistencies encountered in reading.

● Comprehension C
Concept Applications

Who It's For

Comprehension C is designed for students who have completed **Comprehension B2** in the *Corrective Reading* series, and for students whose scores on the Comprehension Placement Test qualify them for entry into the program. These students are probably in grades 6 through 12, and they may even be found in junior college. The program may also be used developmentally for students of average or above-average ability beginning in grade 5.

Students who place in **Comprehension C** have already learned many skills. Specifically, they understand basic logical operations; they can draw conclusions from evidence; their basic vocabularies are reasonably broad; and their recitation and statement-repetition skills are fairly good.

These students, however, have several common skill deficiencies.

▲ Although they are fairly proficient in logical reasoning, they have not mastered reasoning skills to the point where applying them is nearly automatic.

▲ They have trouble learning a new concept or discrimination from written instructions, although the same concept or discrimination would not be difficult to learn if it were presented orally by the teacher.

▲ They are deficient in advanced vocabulary.

▲ They are weak in the mechanics of writing and editing.

▲ They lack facility in extracting information from sources—such as from a written passage or a graph.

▲ They do not have a facility for working independently.

What Is Taught

The objectives for **Comprehension C** are the same as those in **Comprehension B1** and **B2**: namely, to teach and reinforce a substantial amount of information and many reasoning operations. However, the emphasis in **Comprehension C** is on independent application of learned skills. Eventually, the students use the skills to analyze arguments and to respond to propaganda.

The skills that are taught in **Comprehension C** fall into five categories. Three categories teach component skills and are classified as "basic tools." The two remaining categories teach the application of the component skills to higher-order operations and are classified as "higher-order skills." The diagram below shows that the basic tools skills are cycled into the higher-order, or application, categories.

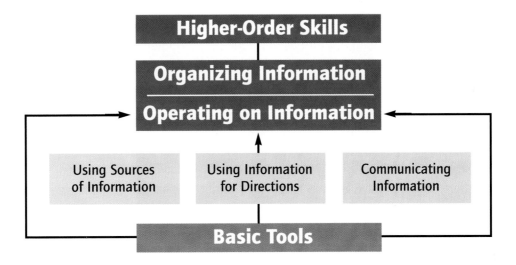

Following is a list of the specific skills taught in each category.

- **Organizing Information** includes the main idea, outlining, specific-general, morals, and visual-spatial organization.
- **Operating on Information** includes deductions, basic evidence, argument rules, *ought* statements, and contradictions.
- **Using Sources of Information** includes basic comprehension passages, words or deductions, maps, pictures and graphs, and supporting evidence.
- **Using Information for Directions** includes writing directions, filling out forms, and identifying contradictory directions.
- **Communicating Information** includes definitions, combining sentences, editing, and obtaining meaning from context.

Because a primary objective of **Comprehension C** is independence, the procedures for presenting new skills (or for reinforcing skills) are different from those of **Comprehension B1** and **B2**. In **Comprehension C,** new skills are presented in the student material. Instead of the teacher reading a script that explains a concept or application, the students read the script and then apply the concept to specific examples in an exercise. The teacher's role is to monitor this process and ask questions to ensure that the students understand what they read.

Outcome Behavior

Students completing **Comprehension C** have some fairly well-developed skills. They are proficient at analyzing arguments. They have a good understanding of the intent of arguments (which is to convince the reader), and they have the skills necessary to be skeptical about how an author has developed an argument. Although they still may have vocabulary deficiencies, they are able to infer the meaning of a word from its context and to decode definitional statements. They haven't had a great deal of practice in the use of reference material; however, they understand the purpose of the "expert testimony" provided by appropriate references. They know the basic procedures for editing and understand how to correct some of the more common writing errors.

In short, students have learned many skills, and these skills are important facilitators of future learning and application. In order for the students to become experienced, proficient, and completely knowledgeable performers, however, they will have to continue developing these skills. **Comprehension C** has provided a solid framework of skills for such development.

Placement Testing

The *Corrective Reading* Decoding Placement Test and the Comprehension Placement Test provide detailed information for the accurate placement of students in SRA's *Corrective Reading* Decoding and Comprehension programs.

> IT IS IMPORTANT TO ADMINISTER THE PLACEMENT TEST TO ALL STUDENTS BEFORE PLACING THEM IN ANY OF THE PROGRAMS.

If you place students in a single-strand sequence, administer the placement test for only that strand (Decoding or Comprehension). If you place students in a double-strand sequence, administer both placement tests. After the Decoding placement is determined, place the students at the same level or at a lower level in the Comprehension strand.

▶ Decoding Placement

The Decoding Placement Test is individually administered and measures each student's reading accuracy and oral-reading rate. Placement takes into account the student's ability to decode words in sentences and stories.

The test has four parts. Students with serious decoding problems are first tested with part I, which is a timed reading passage. Students who perform below specified accuracy and rate criteria are given part II of the test, a series of sentences that the students read aloud. Students who perform above the specified rate and accuracy criteria on part I are given parts III and IV of the test, both of which are timed reading passages.

If a student's performance level is known to be relatively high, you may begin testing with part III of the test. If you don't have accurate information about a student's performance level, which frequently occurs when students have been in reading programs that do not require oral responding, begin testing with part I.

A reproducible copy of the Decoding Placement Test and details on how to administer it appear in Appendix A at the end of this guide.

A description of possible Decoding program sequences and a comparison of placement in SRA's *Corrective Reading* Decoding programs and SRA's *Reading Mastery* series appear in Appendix C at the end of this guide.

Comprehension Placement

The Comprehension Placement Test consists of two parts. Part I, an oral test that is individually administered, provides an evaluation of the following skills.

▲ Recitation behavior (repeating orally presented sentences)

▲ Deductions (drawing one conclusion)

▲ Analogies

▲ Basic information (common facts that students should know)

▲ Divergent reasoning skills (stating how things are the same and how they are different)

Part II, a written test that can be administered to groups as well as to individual students, tests the following skills.

▲ Statement-inference skills (determining which word in a sentence is being defined and which words define it)

▲ Rule-application skills

▲ Vocabulary skills

A reproducible copy of the Comprehension Placement Test and details on how to administer it appear in Appendix B at the end of this guide.

Teaching Techniques

The *Corrective Reading* teacher must do two things effectively: manage the students and present the tasks. The following section summarizes the teaching techniques used in SRA's *Corrective Reading* series.

 ## Setup for the Lesson

Assign permanent seats. Lower-performing students and those whose behavior poses problems should be seated directly in front of you so that you can monitor their responses. Students in **Decoding A** must be able to see the display in the Teacher Presentation Book. In **Decoding B1, B2,** and **C,** the teacher sometimes presents a short exercise on the chalkboard or an overhead transparency.

 ## Scripted Presentations

An important feature of the series is that it controls a wide range of details that are essential to successful teaching—the sequence of tasks that constitute a lesson, the instructions given to students, the number and type of examples that are practiced, and the precise steps in the development of each skill. Typically, a skill is first presented in isolation in a tightly structured format, and it is developed until the students are asked to apply the skill, along with others, in a variety of contexts.

To control these details, the daily lessons are scripted. What the teacher says for each activity and how the teacher corrects mistakes are specified. The scripts have been designed to ensure a smooth and precise presentation.

These are the typefaces used in the Teacher Presentation Books in the Decoding and Comprehension programs:

- ■ This blue type indicates what the teacher says.
- ■ (This type indicates what the teacher does.)
- ■ *This italic type shows the students' response.*

The following exercise, from **Comprehension A,** Lesson 35, shows how the type is used.

━━━EXERCISE 8━━━

OPPOSITES
The next Thinking Operation is **Opposites.**

1. If something is **not going up,** it's (pause; signal) *going down.*

   To correct:
   a. My turn. If something is **not going up,** it's **going down.**
   b. Your turn. (Repeat step 1.)

2. If something is **quiet,** it's **not** (pause; signal) *noisy.*

   If something is **not empty,** it's (pause; signal) *full.*

   (Repeat step 2 until firm.)

   > ***Individual test***
   > Call on individual students to do step 1 or part of step 2.

3. Let's do some more opposites.
4. Everybody, if something is **not young,** it's (pause; signal) *old.*

   If something is **not short,** it's (pause; signal) *long.* (Repeat step 4 until firm.)

5. If something is **dry,** it's **not** (pause; signal) *wet.*
6. (Repeat steps 1–5 until firm.)

   > ***Individual test***
   > Call on individuals to do steps 1, 2, 4, or 5.

Lesson 35, Exercise 8 from Comprehension A TPB A2

In addition to controlling program sequences, scripted presentations have other advantages:

- Scripted directions allow teachers to present a number of examples quickly. Some teachers might present wordy explanations that do not permit the time to present many examples.

- Scripted directions standardize the wording from example to example so that students will not be confused by varying instructions.

- Teacher training is simplified, because trainers can work on common presentation problems.

- Scripts provide efficient correction procedures that contain few words and build on what the students have already been taught.

- The time spent on each activity is controlled; therefore, a more effective development of a range of skills is guaranteed.

 # Formats

Formats are used throughout the programs to make the presentation of similar activities easier for the teacher and the students. A format is an exercise structured so that the same form can be used to accommodate similar tasks. By changing some details of an exercise that is formatted, another exercise can be created. Formats simplify the presentation of similar activities, because the teacher's behavior remains basically the same for all examples of a given format. Once the teacher learns the format, handling various examples is relatively easy. Formatted exercises help students to understand what is being presented, because the directions and wording are the same for all examples of a particular format. The format, therefore, functions as a prompt for applying a skill to new examples.

• A large blue dot preceding an exercise heading indicates the first appearance of a format. A double vertical rule indicates a correction procedure.

The following example is the same format as the one shown in the preceding section, Scripted Presentations. A different exercise has been created by changing the examples given in the format.

EXERCISE 12

OPPOSITES
The next Thinking Operation is **Opposites.**
1. If something is **not noisy,** it's (pause; signal) *quiet.*
   To correct:
   a. My turn. If something is **not noisy,** it's **quiet.**
   b. Your turn. (Repeat step 1.)
2. If something is **short,** it's **not** (pause; signal) *long.*
   If something is **wet,** it's **not** (pause; signal) *dry.* (Repeat step 2 until firm.)

> *Individual test*
> Call on individual students to do step 1 or part of step 2.

3. Let's do some more opposites.
4. Everybody, if something is **not full,** it's (pause; signal) *empty.*
   If something is **not old,** it's (pause; signal) *young.*
   (Repeat step 4 until firm.)
5. If something is **going down,** it's **not** (pause; signal) *going up.*
6. (Repeat steps 1–5 until firm.)

> *Individual test*
> Call on individual students to do step 1, 2, 4, or 5.

Lesson 36, Exercise 12 from Comprehension A TPB A2

Included in the format is the specification of a correction procedure for the mistakes that students most likely will make when introduced to that format. Correction procedures are usually specified the first two or three times a format appears; then the correction is dropped from the format, but it should still be followed by the teacher when necessary.

Corrections

All students make mistakes. Mistakes provide valuable information about what kinds of difficulties students are having. Knowing how to correct effectively is essential to good teaching. Two kinds of correction procedures are used in *Corrective Reading*—general correction procedures and specified correction procedures. (See pages 76–81.)

Pacing the Exercises

Because a great deal of information must be taught during the daily presentation, it is important for the teacher to move quickly, but not to rush the students so much that they make mistakes. To ensure a smoothly paced lesson, the teacher should become familiar with the exercises before presenting them. The teacher must be able to present them without having to refer to the page for every word. Lines should be said quickly and instructions should be concise.

Fast pacing is important for the following reasons.

- It reduces problems of managing students and maintaining on-task behavior. This has been demonstrated through studies of the relationship between student engagement in tasks and the rate at which the tasks are paced. Faster pacing secures more student interest for a longer period of time, which means that management problems are reduced.

- It results in greater student achievement. With faster pacing, a teacher can cover more material in a fixed amount of time and provide more student practice in that time.

- Many tasks become more difficult when they are presented slowly. Slower pacing places greater memory demands on students. Faster pacing, on the other hand, reduces the memory load by giving students less time to forget and allows students to learn by doing the tasks.

Signals

When tasks calling for a group answer are presented, the entire group should respond on signal. This means that all the students respond in unison when the teacher signals them. By listening carefully to the responses, the teacher can tell both which students make mistakes and which ones respond late, copying those who responded first. As a result, the teacher will be able to correct specific mistakes, maximize the amount of practice, and evaluate the performance of each student.

Here are the rules for effective signaling.

- ■ The teacher should never signal while talking. Talk first, then signal.
- ■ The time interval between the last word of the instructions and the signal should always be about 1 second. Signals should be consistently timed so that students can respond together.

If a student fails to answer when the signal is given, the teacher corrects by saying I have to hear everybody and then returns to the beginning of the task.

If a student responds either before or too long after the signal, the teacher calls attention to the signal and returns to the beginning of the task. For example, if students respond before the signal, say: You've got to wait until I signal. Let's try it again.

Teaching to Low Performers

Often, the teacher will have to repeat tasks to make sure that students are firm (that they can do the task). The teacher must judge whether the group is firm on the basis of the low performers, not the high performers. When the low performers are firm, chances are that all students in the group are firm. Rapidly paced repetitions take very little time; therefore, teaching to the low performers does not substantially slow the progress of the higher performers. The procedure assumes that the performances of students in a particular group are not markedly different.

Individual Turns

At the end of some exercises, individual turns are specified. The teacher repeats certain tasks in the exercise, calling on different students to respond individually. The teacher sees that both high and low performers get a chance to respond. Individual turns provide more precise information about a student's performance than group turns do. For example, a student may be able to say a poem when supported by the group. That student may be unable, however, to say the poem without the group prompts.

Positive Reinforcement

Poor readers typically conclude that learning to read is futile, that it is a punishing activity, that it is intimidating, and that because they will never read well, they should not bother trying. Changing this attitude involves thoroughly restructuring the reading situation. This can be done through program design and the use of positive reinforcement. The reading program must be designed so that the sequence of tasks is readily learnable. Without achievable tasks, students will continue to make many mistakes and, therefore, their negative attitude will not change. The program must provide students with evidence that they are improving to counter their tendency to interpret every mistake as proof of failure. The sequence must be planned so that students realize that there is indeed a purpose, a direction, a development in their reading performance.

Two essential features of the programs' reinforcement system are that students earn points for their low error rates and that they summarize their progress on a chart. These features help to provide a positive focus to the learning activities. The use of reinforcers is an important technique in turning on students, improving their performance, and increasing the likelihood that they will practice the skills taught in the program.

Use of Points

Point schedules are specified for each program. In the Level A and Level B programs, points are awarded for performance on each part of the lesson. In Comprehension C, points are awarded for applying skills, not for the process of acquiring the skills. The following chart shows the activities in each program for which points are awarded.

	DECODING	COMPREHENSION
A	Word-Attack Skills Workbook Exercises Individual Reading Checkouts	Thinking Operations Workbook Exercises Information Fact Games and Mastery Tests
B1 & B2	Word-Attack Skills Group Reading Individual Reading Checkouts Workbook Exercises	Oral Exercises Workbook Exercises Fact Games and Mastery Tests
C	Word-Attack Exercises Group Reading Information Reading Individual Reading Checkouts Workbook Exercises	Independent Work Workbook Exercises Student Book Exercises Fact Games and Mastery Tests

The rules for earning points are specified in the lessons. Following are the directions for earning points in Lesson 1 of **Decoding A.**

We're going to do things together. If you all do a good job, everybody in this group will get 4 points.

You must respond on signal, answer when I give individual turns, follow along when somebody else is reading, and try hard. The group will earn points even if you make mistakes—but everybody must try.

If the group does not do a good job, nobody will get any points.

The point system requires students to record their daily points. Point Charts appear on the inside cover of every **Corrective Reading** Workbook. During different parts of the lesson, students record points in the appropriate boxes of their point charts. Below is a sample Point Chart from **Decoding B1.**

Lesson	A	B	C-1	C-2	D	Bonus		TOTAL
26							=	
27							=	
28							=	
29							=	
30							=	
TOTAL							=	

In **Decoding B1**, students earn points for Word Attack (Box A), Group Reading (Box B), Individual Reading Checkout (Box C-1), Timed Reading Checkout (Box C-2), and Workbook Exercises (Box D).

The maximum possible points students can earn for each **Decoding B1** lesson, not counting bonus points, is 20 points. If you teach five lessons a week, a student can earn a maximum of 100 points, not counting bonus points. The point totals for each five-lesson block can be used as an objective basis for awarding grades. To give students a weekly grade, you might choose to use something like the following grading system.

91–100 points	A
81–90 points	B
71–80 points	C
70 points or less	needs work

This grading system is objective and might represent the student's first opportunity to earn an A grade in a school situation that requires excellent performance. The A is a strong reinforcer for many students.

Points also can be used for contingencies other than grades. For instance, you may arrange a special activity for students who earn a specified number of points. Students may also earn tangible reinforcers, such as stickers or decals.

The point system also contains a provision for awarding bonus points. This bonus points provision permits you to deal with special problems. Early in the program, you may award bonus points to students who get to their seats on time, have their material ready for the lesson, or exhibit other behavior that shows their readiness to learn. You may also use bonus points for success on any activity that is especially difficult for the students.

 Adjusting Teaching Techniques

It is more important to follow the techniques described in the previous section with lower-performing students than with higher-performing students. If higher-performing students are not brought to a 100 percent accuracy criterion on every task, their overall performance probably will not suffer appreciably. Neither will their performance suffer if the teacher does not return to the beginning of a list following a mistake or if the teacher does not use elaborate reinforcement procedures.

This does not mean that a teacher working with students who are placed in a Level C program should drop the techniques of signaling, pacing, correcting errors, and reinforcing. The teacher should move as fast as students are capable of learning. The teacher should use signals but should not be overly concerned if students do not respond exactly on signal. The teacher should pay close attention to students' Workbook and oral reading performance, using these as guides.

When working with lower-performing students, especially in Levels A and B, the teacher should follow the specified teaching techniques very closely.

Practicing Signals and Correction Procedures

This section is designed for practice in executing signals and correcting different kinds of mistakes.

 Signal Practice

The **hand-drop, audible,** and **point-touch signals** are used in both the Decoding and the Comprehension programs. The sound-out signal is used only in **Decoding A.** The sequential-response signal is used primarily in the Comprehension programs.

The Hand-Drop Signal

This signal is used for tasks that are presented orally. The following exercise is from **Comprehension B1,** Lesson 51.

EXERCISE 2

INFORMATION: Body Systems

1. Everybody, name the body system that moves blood around the body. (Signal.) *The circulatory system.*
   Name the body system of muscles. (Signal.) *The muscular system.*
   Name the body system that changes food into fuel. (Signal.) *The digestive system.*
   Name the body system of bones. (Signal.) *The skeletal system.*
   (Repeat step 1 until firm.)
2. Name the very small tubes that connect the veins and arteries. (Pause.) Get ready.

(Signal.) *The capillaries.*
Name the tubes that carry blood away from the heart. (Pause.) Get ready. (Signal.) *The arteries.*
Name the pump that moves the blood. (Pause.) Get ready. (Signal.) *The heart.*
Name the tubes that carry blood back to the heart. (Pause.) Get ready. (Signal.) *The veins.*
(Repeat step 2 until firm.)

Individual test
Repeat steps 1 or 2 with individual students.

Lesson 51, Exercise 2 from Comprehension B1 TPB

To execute the hand-drop signal in steps 1 and 2:

1. Hold your hand out (as if you're stopping traffic) while you are saying the instructions or presenting the question.

2. Continue to hold your hand still for 1 second after you have completed the instructions or the question.

3. Then quickly drop your hand. The students should respond the instant your hand drops.

■ *The Audible Signal*

This signal is used primarily when students are attending to material in the Workbook and not looking at the teacher. The teacher can use any audible method to produce this signal—finger snapping, clapping, or foot tapping. The following exercise is from **Comprehension A**, Lesson 31.

═══════ **EXERCISE 12** ═══════

● **INDUCTIONS**
1. Everybody, touch part B in your Workbook. ✔
2. Let's find out the rule for these triangles. Everybody, touch triangle 1. Move to triangle 2. Triangle 2 is different from triangle 1. Everybody, how is it different? (Signal.) *It's smaller.* Yes, it's smaller.
3. Move to triangle 3. ✔ Everybody, how is triangle 3 different from triangle 2? (Signal.) *It's smaller.* Yes, it's smaller.
4. What happens to the triangles as you go from triangle 1 to triangle 3? (Signal.) *They get smaller.* Yes, they get smaller. So, what's the rule for the triangles? (Signal.) *The triangles get smaller.* (Repeat until firm.) Yes, the triangles get smaller.

Lesson 31, Exercise 12 from Comprehension A TPB A1

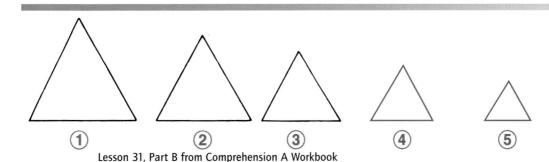

① ② ③ ④ ⑤
Lesson 31, Part B from Comprehension A Workbook

To execute the audible signal in steps 2, 3, and 4:

1. Say the instructions quickly.

2. Pause 1 second.

3. Clap. Students should respond the instant that you clap. (Note that in place of the clap, any audible signal is acceptable.)

Following is a word reading exercise from **Decoding B1,** Lesson 58. In this exercise, students read a random list of words, each with an underlined part. The underlined part may be an ending, a letter combination, or a single letter. This activity serves as an ongoing review of the sounds of the letters and letter combinations. For each word, students first say the sound for the underlined part, then read the word.

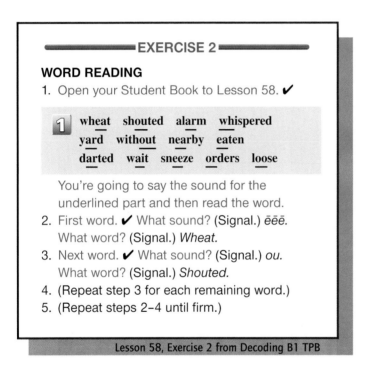

Lesson 58, Exercise 2 from Decoding B1 TPB

Students are looking at the words in their Student Book. Use an audible signal (a snap, clap, or tap) to indicate when they should respond. The pattern is the same for all words.

To execute the signal in step 3:

1. Next word. Check that students are touching the word.

2. What sound? Pause 1 second. Signal. Students should respond the instant that you signal.

3. What word? Pause 1 second. Signal.

Maintain a rapid pace. The steps for each word should take no more than about 3 seconds.

The Point-Touch Signal

This signal is used when pointing to words or symbols in the presentation book or on the chalkboard. The following exercise is from **Decoding B2**, Lesson 7. In this exercise, the teacher writes a list of words on the chalkboard (or on an overhead transparency). After the students read each word in the list, the teacher then changes each word by adding specified endings.

═══════ EXERCISE 1 ═══════

ENDINGS BUILDUP

1. Print in a column on the board: **skip, lean, stare, remember.**

2. For each word:
   (Point to the word.) What word? (Signal.)
3. (Change the list to: **skipped, leaned, stared, remembered.** Repeat step 2.)
4. (Change the list to: **skipping, leaning, staring, remembering.** Repeat step 2.)
5. (Change the list to: **skipped, leaning, stare, remembered.** Repeat step 2.)

Individual test
Call on individual students to read all the words in the column.

Lesson 7, Exercise 1 from Decoding B2 TPB

To execute the point-touch signal in step 2:

1. Hold your finger in front of the word, about an inch away from the chalkboard. Be careful not to cover any part of the word or obscure it from any student's view.

2. As you point, say What word?

3. Pause 1 second.

4. Signal by tapping in front of the word. Students should respond the instant you signal.

The Sound-Out Signal

This signal provides timing for students as they sound out the parts of a word. It is used in **Decoding A** to teach new words. The following sample is from **Decoding A**, Lesson 3.

Task G Me

1. (Point to **m**.) What sound? (Touch under **m**.) *mmm.*
2. (Point to **e**.) What sound? (Touch under **e**.) *ēēē.*
3. (Touch the ball of the arrow.) My turn to sound out this word. (Touch under **m, e** as you say:) **mmmēēē.** (Do not pause between the sounds.)

4. (Touch the ball of the arrow.) Your turn. Sound it out. Get ready. (Touch under **m, e**.) *mmmēēē.* (Repeat until the students say the sounds without pausing.)
5. (Touch the ball of the arrow.) Say it fast. (Slash right, along the arrow.) *Me.* Yes, **me.**

Lesson 3, Task G from Decoding A TPB A1

To execute the signal:

1. Touch the ball of the arrow as you say Sound it out. Get ready.

2. Pause 1 second.

3. Quickly loop your finger to a point just under the first sound of the word.

4. Hold your finger there for 2 seconds (if the sound is continuous). Students should respond as soon as you touch under the sound and continue saying the sound as long as you touch under it.

5. Quickly loop to the next sound and hold for 2 seconds (if the sound is continuous). As soon as you touch under it, students should say this sound without pausing between the sounds.

6. Quickly remove your finger from the page.

The diagram below shows the pointing, looping, and student response. You must loop very quickly from sound to sound. If you loop slowly, students may come in at different times or stop between sounds.

Student response: mmmmmmeeeeeeee

The Sequential-Response Signal

This signal is used in orally presented tasks that require students to produce different responses in a specified sequence. The following sample is an exercise from **Comprehension A,** Lesson 15.

THINKING OPERATIONS

=====EXERCISE 1=====

- **BASIC EVIDENCE: Using Facts**

The first Thinking Operation today is **Basic Evidence.**

1. You're going to use two facts to explain things that happened. These are the only facts you can use. (Hold up one finger.) First fact. The man was very strong. Say it. (Signal.) *The man was very strong.* (Repeat until firm.)
   (Hold up two fingers.) Second fact. The plane had a broken engine. Say it. (Signal.) *The plane had a broken engine.* (Repeat until firm.)

2. Everybody, say those facts again. (Hold up one finger.) First fact. *The man was very strong.* (Hold up two fingers.) Second fact. *The plane had a broken engine.* (Repeat until the students say the facts in order.)

Lesson 15, Exercise 1 from Comprehension A TPB A1

To execute the signal in step 1:

1. Hold up one finger while you are presenting the statement.

2. Pause for 1 second after you say Say it. Don't move your finger or your hand during the pause.

3. Quickly move your finger (or your hand). Students should respond the instant your finger (hand) moves.

4. Then follow the same procedure with two fingers.

The sequential-response signal is also used in step 2.

Correction Procedures Practice

A correction procedure should be presented to the entire group of students, not just to those who made the mistake. Because corrections are not meant as punishment, it is important to present them as just another step in the lesson. Although many correction procedures are specified in the *Corrective Reading* programs, there is one general procedure for correcting just about any mistake that students make.

The General Correction Procedure

The correction procedure involves five steps.

1 Say the answer.

2 Repeat the task.

3 Back up in the exercise and present the activities in order.

4 Finish the remaining steps in the exercise.

5 Repeat the entire exercise **if** students made more than one or two mistakes.

Step 1: Say the answer. When you say the answer, do it immediately, the moment you hear an incorrect response. For example, if students omit a word in a verbal rule, do not wait until the students have completed trying to say the rule before correcting the error. Say the correct answer as soon as you hear the word omitted. If a student makes a mistake while orally reading a sentence, do not wait until the student completes reading the sentence to correct the error. Say the correct word as soon as you hear the misidentified word.

Step 2: Repeat the task. When you repeat the task, repeat the instructions you gave the students. If you said What word? that's the task you repeat. If you said What's the rule about living things? those are the words you present after saying the correct answer. Do not let the students just repeat the correct answer after you say it. Make sure they respond to the task they missed (i.e., the specific question or instructions).

Step 3: Back up in the exercise and present the steps in order. The purpose of going back in the exercise is to make sure that the students can remember the answer to the task you just corrected. If you only say the answer and then go on, you have no idea whether the correction procedure was effective. If you back up in the exercise and present the activities as they are specified in the Teacher Presentation Book, you'll see if the students remember the correct response. When you come to the step where students previously made the error, they will either make a correct response or make an error. If they answer correctly, you know that they remembered the information. If they answer incorrectly, you know that they didn't and that they need more practice.

When you back up in an exercise, go back at least three tasks (whenever possible). A simple procedure in the Word-Attack Exercises of the Decoding programs is to use the columns or rows of words as markers for going back. If a mistake occurs in the middle of column 3, go back to the beginning of column 3.

Following is a sample exercise from **Comprehension A**, Lesson 17. An error is indicated at step 3.

━━━━━━ EXERCISE 4 ━━━━━━

DEDUCTIONS: With *some*

The next Thinking Operation is **Deductions.**

1. Listen to this rule. **Some** girls are tall. Everybody, say that. (Signal.) *Some girls are tall.*

2. Mary is a girl. So, is Mary tall? (Signal.) *Maybe.* Yes, **maybe** Mary is tall. Again. **Some** girls are tall. Mary is a girl. So (pause; signal), *maybe Mary is tall.*

3. How do you know that maybe Mary is tall? (Signal.) *Because some girls are tall.** (Repeat step 3 until firm.)

Lesson 17, Exercise 4 from Comprehension A TPB A1

---

*Mistake occurs here.

Students say *Because Mary is a girl.*

The students miss the task: How do you know that maybe Mary is tall? Here are steps 1–3 of the general correction procedure.

---

1. (Say the answer.) Because some girls are tall.

2. (Repeat the task.) How do you know that maybe Mary is tall? (Signal.) *Because some girls are tall.*

3. (Return to step 1 of the exercise and present the steps in order.)

If a student makes a mistake in the middle of a sentence, use the same correction procedure. In the following example from Decoding B2, an **X** indicates where a student misidentifies a word.

> X
>
> Hurn's nose, like noses of all wolves, was very keen.

Here are steps 1–3 of the general correction procedure.

1. (As soon as you hear the student misidentify the word **noses,** say the correct word.) That word is noses.

2. (Repeat the task.) Touch under the word. ✔ What word? *Noses.*

3. (Direct the student to return to the first word in the sentence and read the sentence again.)

The correction procedure is effective because it ensures that the student is able to respond to the task or specific detail that was missed WITHIN THE CONTEXT IN WHICH THE MISTAKE ORIGINALLY OCCURRED. When you get information that the student is able to perform within this context, you know that you have provided an adequate correction, one that will help shape the student's skills. If you merely say the answer and then go on, you are probably doing little to change the student's reading behavior or skills.

Step 4: Finish the remaining steps in the exercise. Following a correction (saying the answer, repeating the task, backing up in the exercise), you finish the exercise. If students make another error, use steps 1–3 of the correction procedure.

Step 5: Repeat the entire exercise if students made more than one or two mistakes. At the end of the exercise, you evaluate whether or not to present step 5 of the correction, repeating the entire exercise. The purpose of this step is to make sure that the students can do all steps in the exercise without making a mistake. By looking at the presentation from the standpoint of the students, you can appreciate why this step is important. If students make frequent mistakes in an activity, they do not see how the pieces fit together. For them, the activity has not been a series of steps that link together to form a whole. It has been only parts that may have been arbitrarily put together.

The goal is for students to go through an activity at a good pace, making no errors. Therefore, if only one or two errors occur in an exercise, and if these mistakes have been corrected, the students have received a good demonstration of how that activity works. But if there were many mistakes in the activity, you should repeat the entire exercise.

If students continue to have difficulty with an exercise, a good procedure is to go on to the next activity in the lesson, then return to the exercise in which the errors occurred and present the exercise from the beginning. Students will perform better on the repeated exercise if they know that you will return to it. Establish a clear expectation: We got through that list, but we're going to come back to it later. Make sure you remember all those words.

Remember, learning is accelerated when students are able to perform perfectly on activities in the program after errors are corrected. Students learn far more slowly if they do not receive clear demonstrations of what perfect performance is.

■ *Specified Correction Procedures*

In both the Decoding and Comprehension programs, specified correction procedures are indicated for some of the more troublesome and predictable mistakes that students will make. These correction procedures usually include the same steps as the general correction procedure (say the answer; repeat the task; back up in the exercise, and start over). The specified correction procedures, however, provide additional steps. These additional steps occur after step 2 in the general procedure.

1 Say the answer.

2 Repeat the task.

* * *

3 Back up in the exercise and present the activities in order.

4 Finish the remaining steps in the exercise.

5 Repeat the entire exercise if students made more than one or two mistakes.

The interpolated step is indicated with **asterisks.** That step varies from program to program; however, it always occurs after you say the answer and repeat the task.

- ■ The interpolated step in **Decoding A** may be to tell the students to sound out the word.

- ■ The interpolated step in **Decoding B1** through **C** may be to tell the students to spell the word.

■ The interpolated step in **Comprehension A** may be to say the correct response with the students (lead).

■ The interpolated step in **Comprehension B1** and **B2** may be to tell the students to say the rule that governs the correct answer.

The rest of the correction procedure remains the same. Following the interpolated step, you back up and present the missed item within the context in which the mistake originally occured (step 3). You then finish the remaining steps in the exercise (step 4).

Correction Reminder: Follow these steps to correct all word-identification errors during Word-Attack Skills.

1. The word is ———.
2. What word? (Signal.)
3. Spell ———. (Signal for each letter.)
   What word? (Signal.)
4. Go back to the first word in the (row/column). ✔ What word? (Signal.)

The following example is from **Decoding B1**, Lesson 11. In this lesson, the specified correction procedure is displayed in a note to the teacher at the beginning of the Student Book Word-Attack Skills exercise. Step 3 of the correction procedure tells the teacher to direct students to spell the word.

════════ **EXERCISE 6** ════════

● **WORD READING**

Task A   Irregular Words

1. Touch the first word in part 4. ✔

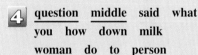

4 | question   middle   said   what
you   how   down   milk
woman   do   to   person

2. That word is **question.** What word? (Signal.) *Question.*
3. Spell **question.** (Signal for each letter.) What word? (Signal.) *Question.*
4. Next word. ✔ That word is **middle.** What word? (Signal.) *Middle.*
5. Spell **middle.** (Signal for each letter.) What word? (Signal.) *Middle.*

Task B

1. This time you will just read the words. Go back to the first word. ✔ What word? (Signal.) *Question.*
2. Next word. ✔ What word? (Signal.) *Middle.*
3. (Repeat step 2 for each remaining word.)

Lesson 11, Exercise 6 from Decoding B1 TPB

To correct a mistake on the word **middle** in step 2 of Task B, follow these steps.

---

1. (Say the answer:) The word is **middle.**

2. (Repeat the task:) What word? (Signal.)
   Middle.

3. Spell **middle.** (Signal for each letter.) What
   word? (Signal.) *Middle.*

4. (Back up in the exercise and present the
   words in order:) Go back to the first word in
   the row. ✔ What word? (Signal.) *Question.*

5. Next word. ✔ What word? (Signal.) *Middle.*

   Next word. ✔ What word? (Signal.) *Said.*

   Next word. ✔ What word? (Signal.) *What.*

In the preceding correction procedure, the spelling step is added to the general correction. The reason for the spelling step is that students may not be attending to the specific arrangement of letters in the word. The spelling step prompts them to attend to the letter details.

Practice using the general correction procedure. If you become facile with this procedure, you will find that the steps in the specified correction procedures are easy to follow. Use this guideline: if you don't remember the specific correction, use the general correction procedure. It will work. The specific correction procedures focus on important details of what and how the students are learning and should be followed when possible, but if in doubt, use the general correction procedure.

Lesson Parts and Feedback Measures

Following is a list of the lesson parts in each program. The activities marked with asterisks provide the most critical feedback on students' mastery of skills.

▶ Decoding Lesson Parts

Decoding A

1. Word-Attack Exercises
2. Awarding points for word-attack
3. Workbook Exercises*
4. Workcheck
5. Awarding points for Workbook
6. Individual Reading Checkouts*
7. Awarding points for Individual Reading Checkouts
8. Totaling points for the lesson

Decoding B1, ■ Decoding B2

1. Word-Attack Exercises
2. Awarding points for word-attack
3. Group Reading activities*
4. Awarding points for Group Reading
5. Individual Reading Checkouts*
6. Awarding points for Individual Reading Checkouts
7. Workbook Exercises*
8. Workcheck
9. Awarding points for Workbook
10. Totaling points for the lesson

■ *Decoding C*

Lessons 1–54

1. Word-Attack Exercises
2. Awarding points for Word-Attack
3. Group Reading*
4. Awarding points for Group Reading
5. Individual Reading Checkouts*
6. Awarding points for Individual Reading Checkouts
7. Workbook Exercises*
8. Workcheck
9. Awarding points for Workbook
10. Totaling points for the lesson

Regular Lessons 56–124

1. Workcheck of preceding lesson's Workbook Exercises
2. Awarding points for preceding lesson's Workbook
3. Totaling points for preceding lesson
4. Word-Attack Skills
5. Group Reading*
6. Awarding points for Group Reading
7. Word-Attack Skills for Information passage
8. Group Reading of Information passage*
9. Awarding points for Group Reading of Information passage
10. Workbook Exercises (as homework)*

Checkout Lessons 55–125

(Every fifth lesson beginning with Lesson 55)

1. Workcheck of preceding lesson's Workbook Exercises
2. Awarding points for preceding lesson's Workbook
3. Totaling points for preceding lesson
4. Word-Attack Skills for in-program Information passage
5. Group Reading of in-program Information passage*
6. Awarding points for Group Reading of Information passage
7. Individual Reading Checkouts of an entire story*
8. Awarding points for Individual Reading Checkouts
9. Workbook Exercises (as homework)*

● Comprehension Lesson Parts

■ *Comprehension A*

Regular Lessons

1. Thinking Operations (oral exercises)
2. Awarding points for Thinking Operations
3. Workbook Exercises*
4. Workcheck
5. Awarding points for Workbook
6. Information exercises (oral)
7. Awarding points for Information exercises
8. Totaling points for the lesson

Fact Game Lessons

1. Fact Game
2. Awarding points for Fact Game
3. Workbook Exercises*
4. Awarding points for Workbook
5. Totaling points for the lesson

■ *Comprehension B1,* ■ *Comprehension B2*

Regular Lessons

1. Oral Exercises

2. Teacher-directed Workbook Exercises

3. Awarding points for oral exercises and teacher-directed Workbook Exercises

4. Independent Workbook Exercises*

5. Workcheck

6. Awarding points for Workbook Exercises

7. Totaling points for the lesson

Fact Game/Mastery Test Lessons

1. Fact Game

2. Awarding points for Fact Game

3. Mastery Test*

4. Workcheck

5. Awarding points for Mastery Test

6. Totaling points for the lesson

■ *Comprehension C*

Regular Lessons

1. Oral Exercises

2. Teacher-directed Workbook and Student Book Exercises

3. Independent Workbook and Student Book Exercises*

4. Workcheck

5. Awarding points for independent Workbook Exercises

Fact Game/Mastery Test Lessons

1. Fact Game
2. Awarding points for Fact Game
3. Mastery Test*
4. Workcheck
5. Awarding points for Mastery Test
6. Totaling points for the lesson

Firm-Up Procedures

The following points summarize what the teacher can do about some unacceptable performance patterns.

Students continue to have trouble with a particular skill that has been taught. The skill may not have been taught adequately. Reteach.

Students consistently miss items of a given type in the Workbook. The item type should be retaught by reviewing previous exercises in the track. The teacher should not continue to permit students to make the same kinds of mistakes day after day.

A student (or a few students) in the group are responsible for most of the errors. Either additional instruction should be provided, or the student(s) should be moved to another group or program.

Mistakes seem to result from carelessness rather than from poor understanding. The teacher can award bonus points (1 or 2) as incentives for students not to make mistakes on the type of item that is chronically missed.

The group consistently fails to meet criteria for earning points. The lessons should be repeated from the point at which students began to fail to meet criteria.

Practice Lessons

This section presents sample lessons from the *Corrective Reading* Decoding and Comprehension programs. The lessons have been selected to show a range of skills taught. The contrast of early lessons with later lessons shows how the programs shift from highly structured teacher presentations to presentations that require more independent use of the skills that have been taught.

Practice teaching the sample lessons from the various programs. Repeat the formats until you can present them quite rapidly with a smooth flow from step to step. Use the appropriate signals. Move from exercise to exercise without pausing between them.

Assume that students will make mistakes at different points in the exercises. Use either the correction procedure specified in the exercise or apply the general correction procedure for correcting errors (see page 76).

▶ Sound Pronunciation

If you teach one of the Decoding programs, you should know the sound for each symbol. Practice the sounds in the sound pronunciation guide. (Note that not all the sounds are taught in every program.) Make sure you can pronounce the sounds for the letters and letter combinations correctly.

Be particularly careful with the sounds that are identified as stop sounds. There should be no vowel sound audible when you say these sounds. Don't say "cuh" for **c.** The sound for **c** is unvoiced. Say the word **sack.** The last sound you say when you pronounce the word is the appropriate sound for **c** (as well as for **k** and **ck**). Similarly, the sound **b** is not pronounced "buh." If you pronounce it this way, students will have difficulty "blending" this sound with other sounds in a word. The pronunciation for **b** is the sound that occurs at the end of the word **hub.** (Whisper the rest of the word and say the **b** sound aloud.)

Although the sounds for many letter combinations are continuous, say these sounds fairly quickly. The sound for **al** is the same as if you say the word **all** aloud at a normal speaking rate, not "alllll." The sound for **ar** is the same as if you say the word **are** aloud, not "arrrrr."

Sound Pronunciation Guide

Sound	As In	Type
a	and/ate	continuous
b	bag	stop
c	cat	stop
d	dad	stop
e	end	continuous
	me	continuous
f	fit	continuous
g	go	stop
h	he	stop
i	if	continuous
	bite	continuous
j	jump	stop
k	kid	stop
l	lip	continuous
m	mat	continuous
n	not	continuous
o	odd	continuous
	note	continuous
p	pan	stop
qu	quit	continuous
r	run	continuous
s	sat	continuous
t	tap	stop
u	up	continuous
	use	continuous
v	van	continuous
w	will	continuous
x	ox	continuous
y	yell	continuous
z	zip	continuous
ai	pain	continuous
al	fall	continuous
ar	art	continuous
au	auto	continuous
aw	awful	continuous

Sound	As In	Type
ce, ci	ice, icing	continuous
ch	chip	stop
cial	special	continuous
ck	sack	stop
ea	eat	continuous
	head	continuous
ee	feel	continuous
er	her	continuous
ge, gi	age, aging	stop
igh	night	continuous
ing	sing	continuous
ir	stir	continuous
kn	knot	continuous
oa	boat	continuous
oi	boil	continuous
ol	cold	continuous
oo	soon	continuous
or	fort	continuous
ou	out	continuous
oul	could	continuous
sh	ship	continuous
tch	catch	stop
th	them	continuous
tial	partial	continuous
tion	nation	continuous
ur	burn	continuous
ure	pure	continuous
(w)a	w<u>a</u>sh	continuous
wh	when	continuous

▶ Decoding A—Lesson 6

Core skills are introduced in this early lesson. Students practice the following skills.

◆ Pronouncing orally presented words so that all sounds are audible (Exercise 1)

◆ Identifying the first and middle sound in orally presented words (Exercises 1 and 5)

◆ Identifying which of two orally presented words has a specified middle sound (Exercises 1 and 5)

◆ Learning a new sound: **fff** (Exercise 2)

◆ Identifying the eight sounds that have been introduced in earlier lessons (Exercise 2)

◆ Orally saying the sounds in words (oral blending) without pausing between the sounds (Exercise 3)

◆ Sounding out and reading word parts, two-sound words, and three-sound words (Exercise 4)

The Workbook Exercises provide practice on the following skills.

■ Writing the letters for sounds dictated by the teacher

■ Sounding out and reading a word part **(at)** and then writing beginning letters to complete words **(mat, sat)**

■ Sounding out and reading word parts, two-sound words, and three-sound words

■ Identifying the sounds of letters and then matching the letters

■ Matching and copying letters

■ Copying words from the list of words previously read

■ Scanning a display of letters for a specific letter that appears repeatedly in the display

Each student also reads aloud words from a Workbook Exercise as an Individual Reading Checkout.

WORD-ATTACK SKILLS

━━━━ EXERCISE 1 ━━━━

PRONUNCIATIONS

Note: Do not write the words on the board. This is an oral exercise.

Task A

1. Listen. His glasses had a gold **rim.** (Pause.) **Rim.** Say it. (Signal.) *Rim.*
2. Next word: **if.** Say it. (Signal.) *If.*
3. (Repeat step 2 for **im, reem, ram.**)
4. (Repeat all the words until firm.)

Task B   It, fit, miff

1. I'll say words that have the sound **ĭĭĭ.** What sound? (Signal.) *ĭĭĭ.* Yes, **ĭĭĭ.**
2. (Repeat step 1 until firm.)
3. Listen: **it, fit, miff.** Your turn: **it.** Say it. (Signal.) *It.* Yes, **it.**
4. Next word: **fit.** Say it. (Signal.) *Fit.* Yes, **fit.**
5. Next word: **miff.** Say it. (Signal.) *Miff.* Yes, **miff.**
6. (Repeat steps 3–5 until firm.)
7. What's the middle sound in the word **fffĭĭĭt?** (Signal.) *ĭĭĭ.* Yes, **ĭĭĭ.** (Repeat step 7 until firm.)

Task C   Mat, meet

1. Listen: **mat.** Say it. (Signal.) *Mat.*
2. I'll say the first sound in the word **mmmăăăt.** (Pause.) **mmm.** What's the first sound? (Signal.) *mmm.* Yes, **mmm.**
3. Say the middle sound in the word **mmmăăăt.** Get ready. (Signal.) *ăăă.* Yes, **ăăă.**

To correct:

a. (Hold up one finger.) **mmm.**
b. (Hold up two fingers.) **ăăă.**
c. What's the middle sound in **mmmăăăt?** (Signal.) *ăăă.* Yes, **ăăă.**
d. (Repeat step 3 until firm.)

4. Listen: **meet.** Say it. (Signal.) *Meet.*
5. I'll say the first sound in the word **mmmēēēt.** (Pause.) **mmm.** What's the first sound? (Signal.) *mmm.* Yes, **mmm.**

6. Say the middle sound in the word **mmmēēēt.** Get ready. (Signal.) *ēēē.* Yes, **ēēē.**
7. One of those words has the middle sound **ēēē.** I'll say both words again: **mat** (pause) **meet.** Which word has the middle sound **ēēē?** (Signal.) *Meet.* Yes, **meet.**

━━━━ EXERCISE 2 ━━━━

SOUND INTRODUCTION

1. (Point to **f.**) This letter makes the sound **fff.** What sound? (Touch.) *fff.*
2. Your turn. Say each sound when I touch it.
3. (Point to **f.**) What sound? (Touch under **f.**) *fff.*
4. (Repeat step 3 for **ē, m, ĭ, r, d, ă, t, s.**)

To correct:

a. (Say the sound loudly as soon as you hear an error.)
b. (Point to the sound.) This sound is _____. What sound? (Touch.)
c. (Repeat the series of letters until the students can correctly identify the sounds in order.)

f e m
i r d
a t s

Individual test

I'll call on different students to say all the sounds. If everybody I call on can say all the sounds without making a mistake, we'll go on to the next exercise. (Call on two or three students. Touch under each sound. Each student says all the sounds.)

━━━━━━━━ EXERCISE 3 ━━━━━━━━

● **SAY THE SOUNDS**

> **Note:** Do not write the words on the board. This is an oral exercise.

1. Listen: **fffēēē.** (Hold up a finger for each sound.)
2. Say the sounds in (pause) **fffēēē.** Get ready. (Hold up a finger for each sound.) *fffēēē.* (Repeat until the students say the sounds without stopping.)
3. Say it fast. (Signal.) *Fee.*
4. What word? (Signal.) *Fee.* Yes, **fee.**
5. (Repeat steps 2–4 for **if, fish, sam, at, me, rim, she, we, ship, fat, miff.**)

━━━━━━━━ EXERCISE 4 ━━━━━━━━

WORD READING

Task A   Eed

1. You're going to read each word. First you sound it out; then you say it fast.
2. (Touch the ball of the arrow for the first word.) Sound it out. Get ready. (Touch under **ee, d.**) *ēēēd.* (Repeat until the students say the sounds without pausing.)
   To correct sound errors:
   a. (Say the correct sound loudly as soon as you hear an error.)
   b. (Point to the sound.) What sound? (Touch.)
   c. (Repeat until firm.)
   d. (Repeat step 2.)
3. Again. Sound it out. Get ready. (Touch under **ee, d.**) *ēēēd.* (Repeat until firm.)

eed

4. (Touch the ball of the arrow.) Say it fast. (Slash right, along the arrow.) *Eed.* Yes, **eed.**
   To correct say-it-fast errors:
   a. (Say the correct word:) **eed.**
   b. (Touch the ball of the arrow.) Say it fast. (Slash right.) *Eed.*
   c. (Return to step 2.)

Task B   Seed

1. (Touch the ball of the arrow for the next word.) Sound it out. Get ready. (Touch under **s, ee, d.**) *sssēēēd.* (Repeat until the students say the sounds without pausing.)
2. Again. Sound it out. Get ready. (Touch under **s, ee, d.**) *sssēēēd.* (Repeat until firm.)
3. (Touch the ball of the arrow.) Say it fast. (Slash right. *Seed.*) Yes, **seed.**
4. (Repeat steps 1–3 for **seem, at, eet, it, if.**)

seed

seem

at

eet

it

if

Task C

1. (Touch the ball of the arrow for the next word.) Sound it out. Get ready. (Touch under **i, m.**) ĭĭĭm. (Repeat until the students say the sounds without pausing.)
2. Again. Sound it out. Get ready. (Touch under **i, m.**) ĭĭĭm. (Repeat until firm.)
3. (Touch the ball of the arrow.) Say it fast. (Slash right.) Im. Yes, **im.**
4. (Repeat steps 1–3 for **am, sa, see, fa.**)

im

am

sa

see

fa

Task D

1. (Touch the ball of the arrow for the first word.) Sound it out. Get ready. (Touch under **f, ee.**) fffēēē. (Repeat until the students say the sounds without pausing.)
2. Again. Sound it out. Get ready. (Touch under **f, ee.**) fffēēē. (Repeat until firm.)
3. (Touch the ball of the arrow.) Say it fast. (Slash right.) Fee. Yes, **fee.**
4. (Repeat steps 1–3 for **fi, fit, fat, feet.**)

fee

fi

fit

fat

feet

EXERCISE 5

PRONUNCIATIONS

> **Note:** Do not write the words on the board. This is an oral exercise.

1. Listen: **sam.** Say it. (Signal.) *Sam.*
2. I'll say the first sound in the word **sssăăămmm.** (Pause.) **sss.** What's the first sound? (Signal.) *sss.* Yes, **sss.**
3. Say the middle sound in the word **sssăăămmm.** Get ready. (Signal.) *ăăă.* Yes, **ăăă.**

   To correct:
   a. (Hold up one finger.) **sss.**
   b. (Hold up two fingers.) **ăăă.**
   c. What's the middle sound in **sssăăămmm?** (Signal.) *ăăă.* Yes, **ăăă.**
   d. (Repeat step 3 until firm.)
4. Listen: **seem.** Say it. (Signal.) *Seem.*
5. I'll say the first sound in the word **sssēēēmmm.** (Pause.) **sss.** What's the first sound? (Signal.) *sss.* Yes, **sss.**
6. Say the middle sound in the word **sssēēēmmm.** Get ready. (Signal.) *ēēē.* Yes, **ēēē.**
7. One of those words has the middle sound **ăăă.** I'll say both words again: **sam** (pause) **seem.** Which word has the middle sound **ăăă?** (Signal.) *Sam.* Yes, **sam.**

WORKBOOK EXERCISES

> **Note:** Pass out the Workbooks. Direct the students to open their Workbooks to Lesson 6.

(Award 4 points if the group worked well during the word attack. Then say:) Remember, you can earn 5 points for doing a good job on your Workbook lesson.

EXERCISE 6

SOUND DICTATION

1. Everybody, touch part 1 in your Workbook. ✔ These are the sounds you did before. Say all the sounds once more before you write the letters.
2. Touch the first sound. ✔ What sound? (Clap.) *ĭĭĭ.* Yes, **ĭĭĭ.**
3. Touch the next sound. ✔ What sound? (Clap.) *ēēē.* Yes, **ēēē.**
4. (Repeat step 3 for each remaining sound.)
5. Now you're going to write the letters for the sounds I say. First sound. (Pause.) **fff.** What sound? (Clap.) *fff.* Write it in the first blank. (Check work and correct.)
6. Next sound. (Pause.) **ĭĭĭ.** What sound? (Clap.) *ĭĭĭ.* Write it in the next blank. (Check work and correct.)
7. (Repeat step 6 for **sss, ēēē, d, mmm, t, ăăă, ĭĭĭ, rrr, ēēē, t, sss, ăăă, d, mmm.**)
8. (Check that students can write all the letters without errors.)

EXERCISE 7

● WORD COMPLETION

1. Everybody, touch the first word in part 2. ✔
2. Sound it out. Get ready. (Clap for each sound as the students touch under **a, t.**) *aat.* (Repeat until the students say the sounds without pausing.)
3. Say it fast. (Signal.) *At.* Yes, **at.**
4. You're going to change **at** to say (pause) **mat.** What will it say? (Signal.) *Mat.*
5. The first sound in **mat** is **mmm.** What sound? (Signal.) *mmm.* Write the letter for **mmm** before (pause) **at.** (Check work and correct.)
6. You started with the word (pause) **at.** Now you have the word **mat.** What word did you start with? (Signal.) *At.* Yes, **at.** And what word do you have now? (Signal.) *Mat.* Yes, **mat.**
7. Touch the word on the next arrow. ✔ That word says (pause) **at.**
8. You're going to change **at** to say (pause) **sat.** What will it say? (Signal.) *Sat.*

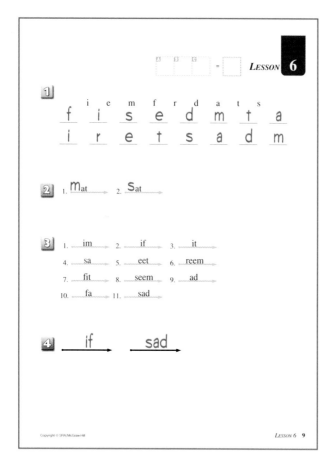

3. Again. Sound it out. Get ready. (Clap for each sound.) *īīīmmm.* Say it fast. (Signal.) *Im.* Yes, **im.**

   To correct errors:
   a. (Say the correct word:) **im.**
   b. What word? (Signal.) *Im.*
   c. You're going to sound it out again. Get ready. (Clap for each sound.) *īīīmmm.*
   d. Say it fast. (Signal.) *Im.*
   e. (Go to the next word.)

4. Touch word two. ✔

5. Sound it out. Get ready. (Clap for each sound as the students touch under **i, f.**) *īīīfff.* (Repeat until the students say the sounds without pausing.)

6. Again. Sound it out. Get ready. (Clap for each sound.) *īīīfff.* Say it fast. (Signal.) *If.* Yes, **if.**

7. (Repeat steps 4–6 for words 3–11.)

Individual test
(Call on each student to read two words in part 3.) Sound out each word and then say it fast. Remember to touch the sounds as you say them. Don't stop between the sounds.

9. The first sound in **sat** is **sss.** So, what do you write before (pause) **at?** (Signal.) *sss.* Yes, **sss.** Do it. (Check work and correct.)

10. You started with the word (pause) **at.** What word do you have now? (Signal.) *Sat.* Yes, **sat.**

━━━━━━━ EXERCISE 8 ━━━━━━━

WORD READING: Workbook

1. Everybody, touch word one in part 3. ✔
2. Sound it out. Get ready. (Clap for each sound as the students touch under **i, m.**) *īīīmmm.* (Repeat until the students say the sounds without pausing.)

   To correct sound errors:
   a. (Say the correct sound loudly as soon as you hear an error.)
   b. Everybody, touch the sound ____. What sound? (Signal.)
   c. (Repeat step 2.)

━━━━━━━ EXERCISE 9 ━━━━━━━

● **WORD COPYING**

1. Everybody, touch part 4. ✔ You're going to write some of the words you just read.
2. The word you're going to write on the first arrow is **if.** What word? (Signal.) *If.*
3. Find **if** and write it just as it is written in part 3. (Check work and correct.)
4. The word you're going to write on the next arrow is **sad.** What word? (Signal.) *Sad.*
5. Find **sad** and write it just as it is written in part 3. (Check work and correct.)

━━━━━━━ EXERCISE 10 ━━━━━━━

MATCHING SOUNDS

1. Everybody, touch part 5. You're going to draw lines to match the letters. Get ready to say the sounds of the letters in the first column.

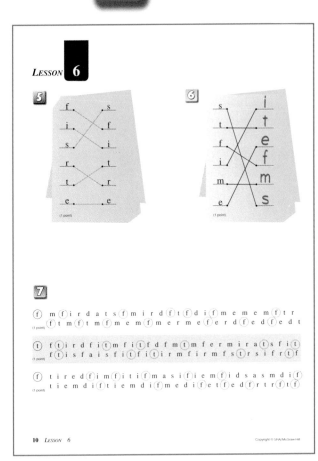

2. Touch the first letter. ✔ What sound?
(Clap.) *fff.*
3. Touch the next letter. ✔ What sound?
(Clap.) *ĭĭĭ.*
4. (Repeat step 3 for **s, r, t, ē.**)
5. Later, you'll draw lines to match the sounds.

═══ EXERCISE 11 ═══

MATCHING AND COPYING SOUNDS
1. Everybody, touch part 6. ✔
2. Later, you'll write letters in the blanks of this matching exercise.

═══ EXERCISE 12 ═══

• **CIRCLE GAME**
1. Everybody, touch part 7. ✔
2. What will you circle in the first two lines?
(Clap.) *fff.*

3. What will you circle in the next two lines?
(Clap.) *t.*
4. What will you circle in the last two lines?
(Clap.) *fff.*
5. Circle the sounds and finish the rest of your Workbook page.

INDIVIDUAL READING CHECKOUTS

═══ EXERCISE 13 ═══

WORKBOOK CHECK
1. (Check each student's Workbook.)
2. (Award points for matching sounds, matching and copying sounds, and the circle game.)
3. (Circle "1 point" below each activity in which a point was earned.)
4. (Write the student's total points in Box B. Maximum = 5 points.)

═══ EXERCISE 14 ═══

WORD-READING CHECKOUT
Study all the words in your Workbook. You'll each get a turn to sound out each word and say it fast. You can earn as many as 4 points for this reading.

If you read all the words with no more than one error, you'll earn 4 points.

If you make more than one error, you do not earn any points. But you'll have another chance to earn 4 points by studying the words some more and reading them again.
(Check the students individually.)
(Record either 4 or 0 points in Box C.)

Lesson Point Total
Tell students to write the point total in the last box at the top of the Workbook page. Maximum for the lesson = 13 points.

Point Summary Chart
Tell students to write this point total in the box for Lesson 6 in the Point Summary Chart.

END OF LESSON 6

1

i　　e　　m　　f　　r　　d　　a　　t　　s

_____ _____ _____ _____ _____ _____ _____ _____ _____

_____ _____ _____ _____ _____ _____ _____ _____ _____

2

1. ⟶ at ⟶   2. ⟶ at ⟶

3

1. ⟶ im ⟶   2. ⟶ if ⟶   3. ⟶ it ⟶

4. ⟶ sa ⟶   5. ⟶ eet ⟶   6. ⟶ reem ⟶

7. ⟶ fit ⟶   8. ⟶ seem ⟶   9. ⟶ ad ⟶

10. ⟶ fa ⟶   11. ⟶ sad ⟶

4

⟶   ⟶

Lesson 6 from Decoding A Workbook

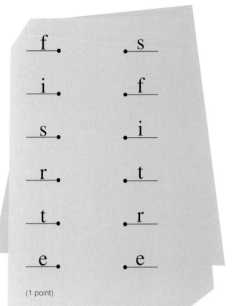

f •   • s

i •   • f

s •   • i

r •   • t

t •   • r

e •   • e

(1 point)

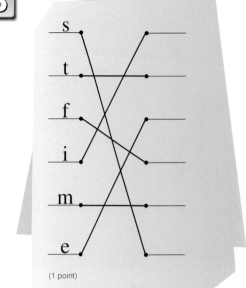

s •

t •

f •

i •

m •

e •

(1 point)

7

(f) m f i r d a t s f m i r d f t f d i f m e m e m f t r
f t m f t m f m e m f m e r m e f e r d f e d f e d t
(1 point)

(t) f t i r d f i t m f i t f d f m t m f e r m i r a t s f i t
f t i s f a i s f i t f i t i r m f i r m f s t r s i f r t f
(1 point)

(f) t i r e d f i m f i t i f m a s i f i e m f i d s a s m d i f
t i e m d i f t i e m d i f m e d i f e t f e d f r t r f t f
(1 point)

Lesson 6 from Decoding A Workbook

▶ Decoding A—Lesson 61

By Lesson 61, students are working on more complicated examples than were presented in Lesson 6. They also review skills introduced in earlier lessons.

These skills are similar to those that were presented in Lesson 6.

◆ Identifying the sounds of letters, now with 34 letters and letter combinations, 12 of which are reviewed in this lesson (Exercise 1)

◆ Pronouncing whole words and individual sounds in words, now including the discrimination of similar vowel sounds, words with difficult consonant blends, and words with endings (Exercise 2)

◆ Reading words, now without first sounding them out (Exercise 3)

◆ Writing the letters and letter combinations for sounds dictated by the teacher (Exercise 4)

These skills were introduced between Lessons 7 and 60.

■ Reading words that are phonically irregular (Exercise 3)

■ Writing words that the teacher dictates (Exercise 5)

■ Adding letters to word parts in the Workbook to complete words that the teacher dictates (Exercise 6)

■ Matching words to word parts and then writing in the missing letters to complete the words (Exercise 7)

■ Reading sentences by identifying each word without sounding it out (Exercise 8)

■ Reading stories by identifying each word without sounding it out (Exercise 9)

■ Orally answering comprehension questions about the story after the teacher re-reads it (Exercise 9)

■ Individually reading the story aloud within specified error and rate criteria (Exercise 11)

WORD-ATTACK SKILLS

EXERCISE 1

SOUND IDENTIFICATION

1. (Point to **o.**) One sound you learned for this letter is the letter name. Everybody, what's that sound? (Touch.) ōōō. Yes, ōōō. What's the other sound? (Touch.) ŏŏŏ. Yes, ŏŏŏ.
2. (Point to **z.**) What sound? (Touch.) zzz. Yes, **zzz.**
3. (Repeat step 2 for **er, th, v, n, j, x, y, ch, u, i.**)

o z er
th v n
j x y
ch u i

Individual test
(Call on two or three students. Touch under each sound. Each student says all the sounds, including two sounds for **o.**)

EXERCISE 2

PRONUNCIATIONS

> **Note:** Do not write the words on the board. This is an oral exercise.

Task A
1. Listen: **chances.** Say it. (Signal.) *Chances.*
2. Next word: **casts.** Say it. (Signal.) *Casts.*
3. (Repeat step 2 for **stopped, fished.**)
4. (Repeat the words until firm.)

Task B   Slum, slim, slam
1. Listen: **slum, slim, slam.** Say those words. (Signal.) *Slum, slim, slam.* (Repeat until firm.)
2. One of those words has the middle sound ĭĭĭ. I'll say the words again: **slum, slim, slam.**
3. Which word has the middle sound ĭĭĭ? (Signal.) *Slim.* Yes, **slim.** Which word has the middle sound ăăă? (Signal.) *Slam.* Yes, **slam.** Which word has the middle sound ŭŭŭ? (Signal.) *Slum.* Yes, **slum.**
4. Listen: **slŭŭŭm.** What's the middle sound in the word **slum?** (Signal.) *ŭŭŭ.* Yes, **ŭŭŭ.** Listen: **slĭĭĭm.** What's the middle sound in the word **slim?** (Signal.) *ĭĭĭ.* Yes, **ĭĭĭ.** Listen: **slăăăm.** What's the middle sound in the word **slam?** (Signal.) *ăăă.* Yes, **ăăă.**
5. (Repeat step 4 until firm.) Good job.

EXERCISE 3

WORD READING THE FAST WAY

1. You're going to read these words the fast way.
2. (For each word:)
   (Touch the ball of the arrow.)
   (Pause.) What word? (Slash right.)
3. (Repeat each list until firm.)

next

under

grabs

of

check

lost

frog

held

you

smelling

just

think

town

lift

damp

belt

after

what

hold

very

Lesson 61 from Decoding A TPB A2

4. (For each word:)
   (Touch the ball of the arrow.)
   (Pause.) What word? (Slash right.)
5. (Repeat the column until firm.)

tramp
funny
blink
lunch
sandy

Note: Pass out the Workbooks. Direct the students to open to Lesson 61.

(Award 3 points if the group worked well during the word attack. Remind the students of the points they can earn in their Workbook lesson.)

EXERCISE 4

SOUND DICTATION

1. I'll say the sounds. You write the letters in part 1 of your Workbook.
2. First sound. Write a letter that says **www** in the first blank. (Check work and correct.)
3. Next sound. Write two letters that go together and say **www.** (Check work and correct.)
4. Next sound. (Pause.) **vvv.** What sound? (Signal.) *vvv.* Write it. (Check work and correct.)
5. (Repeat step 4 for **fff, ththth, shshsh, sss, ch, j, b, ōōō, ăăă.**)
6. (Repeat any sounds the students had trouble with.)

EXERCISE 5

SPELLING FROM DICTATION

1. Touch part 2. ✔ You're going to write words that I dictate.
2. First word: **get.** What word? (Signal.) *Get.* Listen again: **g . . . ĕĕĕ . . . t.** Write it on the first line. (Check work and correct.)
3. Next word: **cup.** What word? (Signal.) *Cup.* Listen again: **c . . . ŭŭŭ . . . p.** Write it on the next line. (Check work and correct.)
4. (Repeat step 3 for **has, born, camp, held, fast.**)

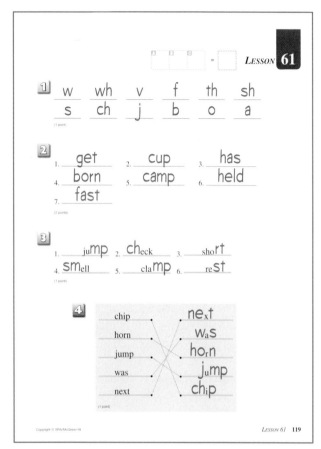

LESSON 61 **119**

============ **EXERCISE 8** ============

SENTENCE READING

1. Everybody, touch sentence 1 in part 5. ✔
2. You're going to read the fast way.
3. First word. ✔ Get ready.
   (Clap for each word. Pause about 2 seconds between claps). *Do . . . you . . . think . . . we . . . can . . . go . . . swimming . . . if . . . it . . . gets . . . sunny?*
4. (Repeat step 3 until the students read the sentence without a mistake.)
5. (Repeat steps 3 and 4 for each remaining sentence. **2. Check with the man at the desk.**
   3. What did they do after dinner?
   4. Did she keep her hands on the wheel?
   5. You can not do math as well as I can.)

Individual test

(Give each student a chance to read one of the sentences. Praise students who read accurately without long pauses.)

============ **EXERCISE 9** ============

STORY READING

Task A

1. Everybody, touch part 6. ✔ You're going to read this story.
2. First word. ✔ Get ready.
   (Clap for each word. Pause about 2 seconds between claps.) *An . . . old . . . truck . . . did . . . not . . . stop . . . well.*
3. (Repeat step 2 until students correctly identify all the words in the sentence in order.)
4. Next sentence. ✔ Get ready.
   (Clap for each word.) *Sandy . . . got . . . in . . . the . . . truck . . . and . . . went . . . to . . . the . . . top . . . of . . . a . . . steep . . . hill.*
5. (Repeat step 4 until students correctly identify all the words in the sentence in order.)
6. (Repeat steps 4 and 5 for each remaining sentence.)
7. (If students miss more than 4 words, repeat the story reading from the beginning.)

============ **EXERCISE 6** ============

WORD COMPLETION

1. Touch the first word in part 3. ✔ Fix it up to say (pause) **jump.** What word? (Signal.) *Jump.* Yes, **jump.** Fix it up. (Check work and correct.)
2. Touch the second word. ✔ Fix it up to say (pause) **check.** What word? (Signal.) *Check.* Yes, **check.** Fix it up. (Check work and correct.)
3. (Repeat step 2 for **short, smell, clamp, rest.**)

============ **EXERCISE 7** ============

MATCHING COMPLETION

1. Everybody, touch part 4. ✔
2. First word. What word? (Signal.) *Chip.*
3. Next word. What word? (Signal.) *Horn.*
4. (Repeat step 3 for **jump, was, next.**)
5. Later, you'll complete the matching words.

LESSON 61

 5

1. Do you think we can go swimming if it gets sunny?
2. Check with the man at the desk.
3. What did they do after dinner?
4. Did she keep her hands on the wheel?
5. You can not do math as well as I can.

6

An old truck did not stop well. Sandy got in the truck and went to the top of a steep hill. Then she went down the hill faster and faster. She said, "I do not think I can stop this truck." A pond was at the end of the street. Now Sandy is sitting in a wet truck with six frogs.

120   LESSON 61   Copyright © SRA/McGraw-Hill

Task B

1. Now I'll read the story and ask questions. Follow along.
2. **An old truck did not stop well. Sandy got in the truck and went to the top of a steep hill.** (Call on a student.) Where did she go? Idea: To the top of a steep hill. (Call on a student.) What is wrong with the truck? Idea: It didn't stop well.
3. **Then she went down the hill faster and faster. She said, "I do not think I can stop this truck."** (Call on a student.) What did she say? *I do not think I can stop this truck.*
4. **A pond was at the end of the street. Now Sandy is sitting in a wet truck with six frogs.** (Call on a student.) Where did the truck go? Idea: Into the pond.
   (Call on a student.) What is Sandy doing now? Idea: Sitting in the truck in the pond with six frogs.

=== EXERCISE 10 ===

WORKBOOK CHECK

1. (Check each student's Workbook.)
2. (Award and circle the points earned for sound dictation, spelling from dictation, word completion, and matching completion.)
3. (Write the student's total points in Box B. Maximum = 5 points.)

=== EXERCISE 11 ===

TIMED STORY-READING CHECKOUT

> **Note:**   For the timed checkouts, you will need a stopwatch.

Study the story. If you read the story with no more than two errors and read it in one minute or less, you'll earn 6 points.

If you make more than two errors, or if you take more than one minute to read the story, you won't earn any points.

If you don't earn points the first time you read the story, you can try again. If you succeed the second time you try, you'll earn 2 points.

(Check the students individually.)

(Record 6, 2, or 0 points in Box C.)

Lesson Point Total

Tell students to write the point total in the last box at the top of the Workbook page. Maximum = 14 points.

Point Summary Chart

Tell students to write this point total in the box for Lesson 61 in the Point Summary Chart.

END OF LESSON 61

_____ _____ _____ _____ _____ _____

_____ _____ _____ _____ _____ _____

(1 point)

2

1. _____   2. _____   3. _____

4. _____   5. _____   6. _____

7. _____

(2 points)

3

1. ____ ju ____   2. ____ eck ____   3. ____ sho ____

4. ____ ell ____   5. ____ cla ____   6. ____ re ____

(1 point)

4

chip •   • x

horn •   • a

jump •   • r

was •   • u

next •   • i

(1 point)

▶ Decoding B1—Lesson 26

By this lesson, the Word-Attack and Group Reading exercises in each lesson have provided practice on the following skills.

◆ Identifying the short sounds for the vowels **a, e, i, o, u**

◆ Identifying two sounds for the vowels **o** and **e**

◆ Identifying the sounds of most common consonants

◆ Identifying the sounds of various letter combinations, including **ee, th, sh, or, ol, ing, ch, wh, er, oo, ea, oa**

◆ Identifying the sounds of letters and letter combinations in words and reading words containing them

◆ Reading common, phonically irregular words, such as **said, was, give, to, what**

◆ Reading silent-**e** words, such as **hope, time, ride**

◆ Reading words with endings, such as **hopped, fatter, mopping, poles, liking, broken, handed**

◆ Reading aloud stories that provide cumulative practice on all the word types introduced, including discriminating between minimally different words **(camp, clamp, tramp, tamp)**

◆ Reading story segments aloud within a specified error limit for each segment

◆ Orally answering comprehension questions about the stories

The Workbook Exercises have provided practice on the following skills.

■ Writing the letters and letter combinations for sounds the teacher dictates

■ Matching words to word parts and then writing in the missing letters to complete the words

■ Reading words with endings and doubled consonants **(hopped, fitting)** and writing the words without endings **(hop, fit)**

■ Reading silent-**e** words with endings **(rider, saving)** and writing the words without endings **(ride, save)**

■ Writing answers to questions about pictures related to the content of a story

■ Writing answers to comprehension questions about a story

■ Copying sentences based on the story

Daily oral reading checkouts have provided practice on reading aloud passages within specified error and rate criteria. Minimum reading rates began at 55 words per minute in Lesson 12 and increased to 70 words per minute by Lesson 26.

The Word-Attack Exercises for Lesson 26 provide practice on the following skills.

● Reading a short word list on the chalkboard (or overhead transparency) that focuses on minimal changes in the words presented (Exercise 1)

● Identifying the sounds of letters or letter combinations in words and then reading the words (Exercise 2)

● Reading silent-**e** words (Exercise 3)

● Reading and spelling aloud new, phonically irregular words and then reading a mixed list of phonically regular and irregular words (Exercise 4)

The Group Reading activity provides practice on reading in context silent-**e** words, words with endings, words containing letter combinations, and phonically irregular words. Immediately after reading each part of the story within a specified error criterion, the students orally answer questions the teacher asks about that part.

Following the reading of the story, students work in pairs and orally read a passage from Lesson 26 within a specified error limit (no more than 2 errors), and a passage from Lesson 25 within specified error and rate criteria (no more than 3 errors, 70 words per minute). Students record points for Lesson 26 Individual Reading Checkouts in Box C-1 (first checkout points) and Box C-2 (second checkout points) of their Point Chart for Lesson 26. (See the sample Point Chart on page 68) Students also keep a record of their performance on the Individual Reading Checkout (second checkout, timed reading) on the Individual Reading Progress Chart in the back of the Workbook. (See the sample chart on page 116.)

The Workbook Exercises provide practice on the following skills.

■ Writing the letters and letter combinations for sounds the teacher dictates (part 1)

■ Reading words with endings and doubled consonants and writing the correctly spelled words without endings (part 2)

■ Writing answers to comprehension questions about a story (part 3)

■ Matching words to word parts and then writing in the missing letters to complete the words (part 4)

■ Copying a sentence based on the story (part 5)

Correction Reminders

Word-Attack Skills. Follow these steps to correct all word-identification errors during Word-Attack Exercises.

1. The word is _____.

2. What word? (Signal.)

3. Spell _____. (Signai for each letter.) What word? (Signal.)

4. Go back to the first word in the row. ✔ What word? (Signal.)

Group Reading Exercises. Follow these steps to correct word-reading errors during Group Reading.

1. (As soon as a student misidentifies a word, say:) The word is _____. Touch under the word. ✔ What word? (Signal.)

2. Go back to the beginning of the sentence and read that sentence again.

WORD-ATTACK SKILLS

Chalkboard

EXERCISE 1

INTERNAL VOWEL CONVERSIONS: ea, oa

1. Print in a column on the chalkboard:
   rear, leaf, mean, ears.

2. For each word: (Point to the word. Pause.)
   What word? (Signal.)

3. (Replace **ea** with **oa** in each word.
   Repeat step 2 for **roar, loaf, moan, oars.**)

4. (Change the list to: **rear, loaf, mean, ears.**
   Repeat step 2.)

5. (Change the list to: **rear, leaf, mean, ears.**
   Repeat steps 2–4 until firm.)

Individual test
Call on individual students to read all the words in the column.

Student Book

EXERCISE 2

WORD READING

1. Open your Student Book to Lesson 26. ✔
   Touch part 1. ✔

1 ran<u>ch</u> fast<u>er</u> <u>ch</u>opped
g<u>oa</u>ts <u>ch</u>ecked h<u>or</u>ses
b<u>e</u>nt <u>s</u>lap l<u>ea</u>ve h<u>ee</u>ls
l<u>oa</u>fers s<u>w</u>am sw<u>i</u>m <u>j</u>ab

You're going to say the sound for the underlined part and then read the word.

2. First word. ✔ What sound? (Signal.) *ch.*
   What word? (Signal.) *Ranch.*
3. Next word. ✔ What sound? (Signal.) *er.* What word? (Signal.) *Faster.*
4. (Repeat step 3 for each remaining word.)
5. (Repeat steps 2–4 until firm.)

EXERCISE 3

WORD READING

1. Touch the first word in part 2. ✔

2 rode named rider safe
makes side tame time

2. What word? (Signal.) *Rode.*
3. Next word. ✔ What word? (Signal.) *Named.*
4. (Repeat step 3 for each remaining word.)

EXERCISE 4

WORD READING

Task A Irregular Words
1. Touch the first word in part 3. ✔

3 <u>Emma</u> <u>anyone</u> <u>nobody</u> <u>good</u>
because let's boss didn't
ready their Flop woman
women milked herself station
question biggest stayed Branch

2. That word is **Emma.** What word? (Signal.)
   Emma. Spell **Emma.** (Signal for each letter.)
   What word? (Signal.) *Emma.*
3. The next word is **anyone.** What word?
   (Signal.) *Anyone.* Spell **anyone.** (Signal for
   each letter.) What word? (Signal.) *Anyone.*
4. The next word is **nobody.** What word?
   (Signal.) *Nobody.* Spell **nobody.** (Signal for
   each letter.) What word? (Signal.) *Nobody.*
5. The next word is **good.** What word? (Signal.)
   Good. Spell **good.** (Signal for each letter.)
   What word? (Signal.) *Good.*

Task B
1. Go back to the first word. ✔ What word?
   (Signal.) *Emma.*
2. Next word. ✔ What word? (Signal.) *Anyone.*
3. (Repeat step 2 for each remaining word.)

EXERCISE 5

WORD-ATTACK SKILLS: Individual Tests

1. (Call on individual students. Each student reads a row. Tally the rows read without error. If the group reads at least 9 rows without making errors, direct all students to record 4 points in Box A of their Point Chart.)

2. (If the group did not read at least 9 rows without errors, do not award any points for the Word-Attack Skills exercises.)

GROUP READING

EXERCISE 6

STORY READING

1. Everybody, touch part 4. ✔

THE RANCHER

There was a big ranch in the West. The rancher who ran this ranch was named Emma Branch. She rode a horse well. She chopped fast, and she swam faster. The men and women who worked for Emma Branch liked her. They said, "She is the best in the West." On her ranch she had sheep and she had cows. There were goats and horses. There was a lot of grass.

The rancher had a lot of women and men working for her. They worked with the sheep and the goats, and they milked the cows. Each worker had a horse. But the rancher's horse was the biggest and the best. It was a big, black horse named Flop.

[1]

Flop got its name because it reared up. When Flop reared up, any rider on it fell down and went "flop" in the grass. But Flop did not rear up when the rancher rode it. Emma Branch bent near Flop's ear and said, "Let's go, Flop." And they went. She did not have to slap the horse. She didn't have to jab her heels and yell at Flop. She just said, "Let's go," and they went like a shot.

Every day, she checked up on the workers to see what they were doing. She checked to see that they were working well and that they were not loafing.

[1]

If a worker was loafing, Emma told the worker, "I will say this for the last time: 'Do not loaf on this ranch any more.' " If a worker was loafing the next time she checked, she said, "Go from my ranch. We do not need loafers here."

The women and men who worked on the ranch said, "When you hear Flop running, you had better be working. If you are not working, you had better get ready to leave this ranch."

But the workers that stayed at the ranch liked to work for Emma Branch. They said, "We like to have Emma on our side. We can see how mean Flop is, and he is very tame when Emma rides him. So it's good to have Emma on your side."

[2]

2. The number after each part of the story shows the number of points each part is worth. After you read each part without making more than 3 errors, I'll ask questions about that part.
3. (Call on a student to read the title.)
4. (Call on individual students, each to read one or two sentences. Praise students who read without making errors. Correct all word-reading errors.)
5. At the end of each part of the story:
   a. (Tell the students the number of errors the group made and whether the group earned points for that part.)
   b. (If the group made more than 3 errors, direct the group to re-read the part.)
6. (After the group reads each part within the error limit, ask the comprehension questions for that part.)

First part:
   a. What was the name of the rancher? *Emma Branch.*
   b. Name some things she did well. Ideas: Rode a horse well, chopped fast, swam faster.
   c. What kind of animals did she have on her ranch? Ideas: Sheep, cows, goats, horses.
   d. Who had the biggest horse? Idea: The rancher; Emma Branch.
   e. What was its name? *Flop.*

Second part:
   a. Why did Flop have the name Flop? Idea: When anyone tried to ride Flop, Flop reared up and the rider went "flop" in the grass.
   b. Did Flop give Emma a hard time? *No.*
   c. What did Emma do every day? Idea: Checked on the workers.

Third part:
   a. What would Emma do if she found a worker loafing for the first time? Idea: Tell the worker not to loaf on the ranch anymore.
   b. What would she do the next time? Idea: Tell the worker to leave the ranch.
   c. Why did the workers think that it was good to have Emma on their side? (Accept reasonable answers.)
7. (After the group has completed reading the story and answering the comprehension questions, tell the students the total number of points to record in Box B of their Point Chart. Maximum = 4 points.)

━━━━━━ EXERCISE 7 ━━━━━━

● **READING CHECKOUTS**

1. (For this part of the lesson, assigned pairs of students work together during the checkouts.)
2. (Each student does two checkouts.)
   a. (First checkout: Students can earn 3 points by making no more than 2 errors on the first part of story 26. Students record points in Box C-1 of their Point Chart.)
   b. (Second checkout: One-minute timed reading. Students can earn 3 points by reading at least **70** words and making no more than 3 errors on the first part of story 25. Students record points in Box C-2 of their Point Chart.)
3. (Direct students to plot their reading rate [words per minute] and number of errors on the Individual Reading Progress Chart.)

Teacher-Directed Activities

━━━━━━ EXERCISE 8 ━━━━━━

WRITING LETTERS FOR SOUNDS

1. Open your Workbook to Lesson 26. ✔ Find part 1. ✔ You're going to write the letter or letters for each sound I say.
2. First sound: **er.** What sound? (Signal.) *er.* Write it.
3. Next sound: **or.** What sound? (Signal.) *or.* Write it.
4. (Repeat step 3 for ĭĭ, **sss, fff, b,** ăăă, ĕĕĕ, ŏŏŏ, **p.**)

Individual test

(Call on a student.) Read the letters you wrote, starting with the first blank.

LESSON **26**

1. er   or   i   s   f
   b   a   e   o   p

2. The words in the first column have endings.
   Write the same words without endings in the second column.
   patted ——— slip
   conning ——— pat
   slipper ——— con

3. Write the answers to these questions:
   1. What was the name of the rancher? Emma Branch
   2. Name 2 things the rancher did well. (rode a horse well; chopped fast; swam faster)
   3. Who had the biggest horse? (the rancher; Emma)
   4. What was the name of the horse? Flop
   5. What did the rancher do every day? (checked up on the workers)

4. Match the words and complete them.
   slap ——— beNt
   bent ——— swIm
   leave ——— sLap
   swim ——— leaVe

5. Copy this sentence:
   Each worker had a horse.
   Each worker had a horse.

28 *LESSON 26*   Copyright © SRA/McGraw-Hill

━━━━━ **EXERCISE 9** ━━━━━

WRITING WORDS WITHOUT ENDINGS

1. Find part 2. ✔ The words in the first column have endings.
2. First word. ✔ What word? (Signal.) *Patted.*
3. Next word. ✔ What word? (Signal.) *Conning.*
4. (Repeat step 3 for **slipper.**)
5. Later, you'll write the same words without any endings.

Independent Student Work

1. Complete your Workbook lesson. If you make no more than 4 errors, you earn 6 points.
2. (After checking the Workbooks, direct students who made no more than 4 errors to record 6 points in Box D of their Point Chart.)

Lesson Point Summary

Tell students to add the points in Boxes A, B, C-1, C-2, and D, plus any bonus points they have earned, and to write this number in the Total box of the Point Chart.

Point Schedule for Lesson 26

Box		Maximum Points
A	Word Attack	4
B	Story Reading	4
C-1	1st Reading Checkout (not timed)	3
C-2	2nd Reading Checkout (timed)	3
D	Workbook	6
Bonus	(maximum = 2)	(2)
Total	(maximum without bonus points)	20

END OF LESSON 26

LESSON 26

1

ranch   faster   chopped
goats   checked   horses
bent   slap   leave   heels
loafers   swam   swim   jab

2

rode   named   rider   safe
makes   side   tame   time

3

Emma   anyone   nobody   good
because   let's   boss   didn't
ready   their   Flop   woman
women   milked   herself   station
question   biggest   stayed   Branch

4

The Rancher

There was a big ranch in the West. The rancher who ran this ranch was named Emma Branch. She rode a horse well. She chopped fast, and she swam faster. The men and women who worked for Emma Branch liked her. They said, "She is the best in the West." On her ranch she had sheep and she had cows. There were goats and horses. There was a lot <u>of</u> grass.

The rancher had a lot of women and men working for her. They worked with the sheep and the goats, and they milked the cows. Each worker had a horse. But the rancher's horse was the biggest and the best. It was a big, black horse named Flop.

[1]

Flop got its name because it reared up. When Flop reared up, any rider on it fell down and went "flop" in the grass. But Flop did not rear up when the rancher rode it. Emma Branch bent near Flop's ear and said, "Let's go, Flop." And they went. She did not have to slap the horse. She didn't have to jab her heels and yell at Flop. She just said, "Let's go," and they went like a shot.

Every day, she checked up on the workers to see what they were doing. She checked to see that they were working well and that they were not loafing.

[1]

46 LESSON 26

If a worker was loafing, Emma told the worker, "I will say this for the last time: 'Do not loaf on this ranch any more.' " If a worker was loafing the next time she checked, she said, "Go from my ranch. We do not need loafers here."

The women and men who worked on the ranch said, "When you hear Flop running, you had better be working. If you are not working, you had better get ready to leave this ranch."

But the workers that stayed at the ranch liked to work for Emma Branch. They said, "We like to have Emma on our side. We can see how mean Flop is, and he is very tame when Emma rides him. So it's good to have Emma on your side."

[2]

LESSON 26

1
_____ _____ _____ _____ _____

_____ _____ _____ _____ _____

2 The words in the first column have endings.
Write the same words without endings in the second column.

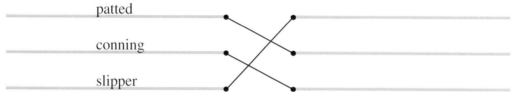

patted

conning

slipper

3 Write the answers to these questions:

1. What was the name of the rancher? _____

2. Name 2 things the rancher did well. _____

_____

3. Who had the biggest horse? _____

4. What was the name of the horse? _____

5. What did the rancher do every day?

_____

4 Match the words and complete them.

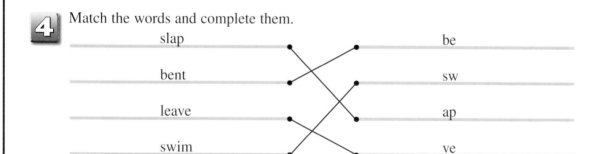

slap   be

bent   sw

leave   ap

swim   ve

5 Copy this sentence:
Each worker had a horse.

_____

Individual Reading Progress Chart
Decoding B1: Lessons 12–35

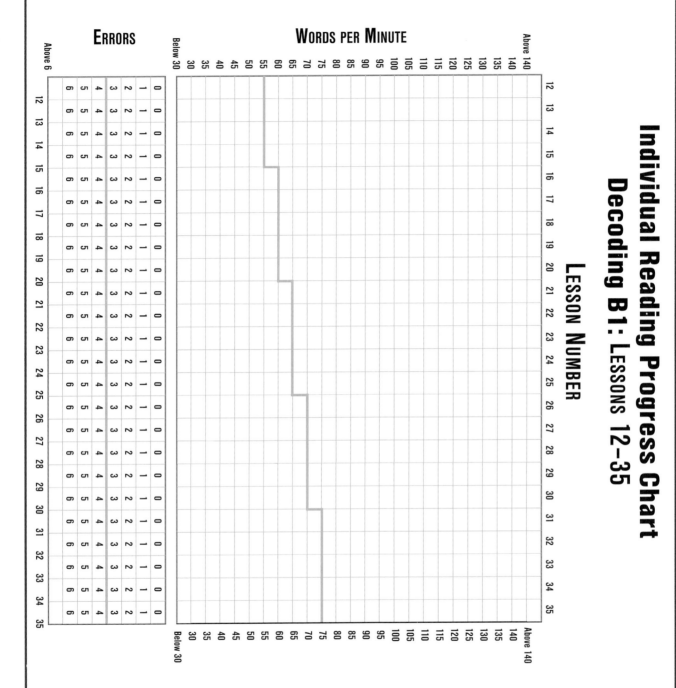

LESSON NUMBER

WORDS PER MINUTE

ERRORS

Individual Reading Progress Chart
Decoding B1: Lessons 36-65

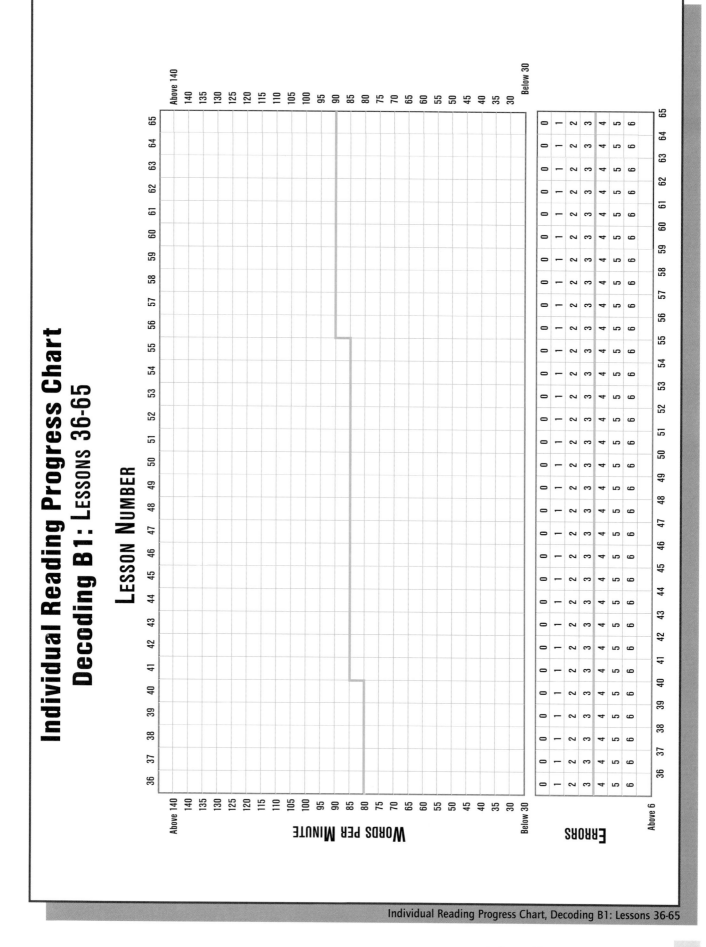

LESSON NUMBER

WORDS PER MINUTE

ERRORS

▶ Decoding B2—Lesson 32

The Word-Attack Exercises for this lesson provide practice on the following skills.

◆ Reading a short word list on the chalkboard (or overhead transparency) that focuses on changes in the endings of the words presented (Exercise 1)

◆ Reading pairs of words that have minimal differences (Exercise 2)

◆ Identifying the sounds of letters or letter combinations in words and then reading the words (Exercise 3)

◆ Reading and orally spelling a new, phonically irregular word and then reading a mixed list of phonically regular and irregular words (Exercise 4)

The story contains a number of words with letter combinations (including **oi,** which is relatively new), words with endings, and compound words. Compared to the story from **Decoding B1** Lesson 26, this story is longer, contains more conventional syntax, and has a more detailed plot.

Following the reading of the story, students work in pairs and read aloud a passage from Lesson 32 within a specified error limit (no more than 2 errors), and a passage from Lesson 31 within specified error and rate criteria (no more than 3 errors, 105 words per minute).

The Workbook Exercises provide practice on the following skills.

■ Sequencing story events (part 1)

■ Writing answers to comprehension questions about a story (part 2)

■ Reading words with endings and then writing the words without endings (part 3)

Correction Reminder
Follow these steps to correct all word-identification errors during Word-Attack Exercises.

1. The word is _____.

2. What word? (Signal.)

3. Spell _____. (Signal for each letter.) What word? (Signal.)

4. Go back to the first word in the [row/column]. ✔ What word? (Signal.)

WORD-ATTACK SKILLS

Chalkboard

=======EXERCISE 1=======

ENDINGS BUILDUP

1. Print in a column on the board: **wash, spill, join.**

2. For each word:
   (Point to the word.) What word? (Signal.)
3. (Change the list to: **washes, spills, joins.** Repeat step 2.)
4. (Change the list to: **washed, spilled, joined.** Repeat step 2.)
5. (Change the list to: **washing, spilling, joining.** Repeat step 2.)
6. (Change the list to: **washes, spilled, joins.** Repeat step 2.)

> **Individual test**
> Call on individual students to read all the words in the column.

Student Book

=======EXERCISE 2=======

WORD CONVERSION

1. Open your Student Book to Lesson 32. ✔

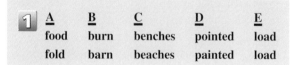

A	**B**	**C**	**D**	**E**
food	burn	benches	pointed	load
fold	barn	beaches	painted	load

Touch part 1. ✔
2. Touch the first word in column A. ✔
   What word? (Signal.) *Food.*
3. Next word. ✔
   What word? (Signal.) *Fold.*
4. (Repeat steps 2 and 3 for the word-pairs in columns B–E.)

=======EXERCISE 3=======

WORD READING

1. Touch the first word in part 2. ✔

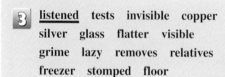

2 soiled cooled eaten watched pounded

What sound? (Signal.) *oy.*
What word? (Signal.) *Soiled.*
2. Next word. ✔
   What sound? (Signal.) *oo.*
   What word? (Signal.) *Cooled.*
3. (Repeat step 2 for each remaining word.)

=======EXERCISE 4=======

WORD READING

1. Touch the first word in part 3. ✔

3 listened tests invisible copper
   silver glass flatter visible
   grime lazy removes relatives
   freezer stomped floor

2. That word is **listened.** What word? (Signal.) *Listened.* Spell **listened.** (Signal for each letter.) *L-i-s-t-e-n-e-d.* What word? (Signal.) *Listened.*
3. Next word. ✔
   What word? (Signal.) *Tests.*
4. (Repeat step 3 for each remaining word.)

=======EXERCISE 5=======

WORD-ATTACK SKILLS: Individual Tests

1. (Call on individual students. Each student reads a row or column. Tally the rows and columns read without error. If the group reads at least 8 rows and columns without making errors, direct all students to record 4 points in Box A of their Point Chart.)
2. (If the group did not read at least 8 rows and columns without errors, do not award any points for the Word-Attack Skills exercise.)

GROUP READING

EXERCISE 6

STORY READING

1. Everybody, touch part 4. ✔

   After you read each part of the story without making more than 2 errors, I'll ask questions about that part.

IRMA TESTS THE INVISIBLE PAINT

Irma had left a nail on the hard paint. When she came back to her lab, the nail was invisible. Slowly she began to realize that the paint had made the nail invisible.

She said to herself, "I will test that paint." She took a coin from her purse and dropped the coin on the paint. Then she watched and waited. After a while, she saw that the coin was starting to turn invisible. It now looked like a glass coin. She could still see it, but it did not look like a copper coin or a silver coin. It looked like a glass coin.

[1]

She dropped it on the floor. "Clink," it went. It sounded like a coin. She took a hammer and hit the coin ten times. She wanted to see what would happen to it now. The coin got flatter and bigger, but it still looked like glass. She said, "I don't believe what is happening."

She set the coin on the paint again and waited. Soon the coin was invisible. Now it didn't look like glass. It didn't look like anything.

"I don't believe it," Irma said to herself. She felt the coin. She could feel the dents that had been made by the hammer.

[1]

Irma closed her eyes and picked up the coin. "It feels like it should feel," she said to herself. Then she opened her eyes and looked at the coin in her hand. It was invisible.

She said, "I must see how this invisible paint works." She got a pot of water and heated it on the stove in her lab. When the water began to boil, she dropped the coin into it. Then she watched to see what would happen.

Slowly she could see the coin begin to form at the bottom of the boiling water. Slowly it became visible. At first the coin looked like glass. Then it began to look like a coin that had been pounded with a hammer.

[1]

She lifted the coin from the boiling water and set it on a sheet of foil. When the coin had cooled, she picked it up and looked at it. She said, "I know that I can remove the invisible paint with boiling water. Now I will try something else."

She took a soiled rag and tore off a small bit. She set the bit of rag on the hard paint. Then she watched as the rag became invisible.

"Now I will see if something else will remove that invisible paint." She took the bit of soiled rag and dropped it in the washtub. Then she turned on the cold water and let it run over the rag.

[2]

The water washed away bits of grime. As each bit of grime left the rag, a spot became visible. But the rest of the rag was still invisible. "Cold water does not seem to work too well," Irma said.

Then she took a can of motor oil from the shelf. She filled a cup with oil and dropped the rag into the cup of oil. Slowly the rag became visible. Irma smiled. She said, "Oil removes the invisible paint."

Now Irma had to think. She could hardly believe what had happened. She went over everything five times. Then she shook her head and said, "It must have happened. I must have made a paint that turns things invisible."

[2]

"Irma," Berta called from upstairs, "what happened to that gallon of ice cream that was in the freezer?"

Irma said, "If it's not in the freezer, you must have eaten it."

Berta yelled, "Well, why didn't you get more? How can we watch TV if we don't have ice cream?"

Lesson 32 from Decoding B2 TPB

> Irma said, "You'll just have to do the best you can."
>
> Berta did not say anything. She stomped back to the living room. As Irma listened to her lazy boarder walking across the floor, she got an idea. She smiled and said to herself, "I think I can have a lot of fun with this invisible paint."
>
> [1]

2. (Call on a student to read the title.)
3. (Call on individual students, each to read one or two sentences. Praise students who read without making errors. Correct all word-reading errors.)
4. (At the end of each part of the story:
   a. Tell the students the number of errors the group made and whether the group earned points for that part.
   b. If one group made more than 2 errors, direct the group to reread the part.)
5. (After the group reads each part within the error limit, ask the comprehension questions for that part.)

First part:
   a. How did she test the paint? Idea: She dropped a coin on the paint.
   b. How did the appearance of the coin change after a while? Idea: It looked like a glass coin.

Second part:
   a. How did the coin change when she hit it with a hammer? Idea: It became flatter and bigger.
   b. When she returned the coin to the paint, what happened to it? Idea: It became invisible.

Third part:
   How did she make the coin reappear? Idea: She dropped the coin into boiling water.

Fourth part:
   a. She found one way to make the invisible things visible again. What was that? Idea: To drop them in boiling water.
   b. She was going to test another way. So she made something else invisible. What was that? Idea: A bit of a soiled rag.
   c. What did she do with the rag when it was invisible? Idea: Put it in the washtub and ran cold water over it.

Fifth part:
   a. How did the water change the rag? Idea: Where it washed away bits of grime, spots became visible.
   b. What did she soak the rag in next? Idea: Motor oil.
   c. What happened to the rag? Idea: It became visible.

Sixth part:
   a. What was Berta complaining about? Idea: She wanted ice cream.
   b. What was Irma thinking at the end of this story? Idea: That she could have fun with the paint.
   c. How could she have fun with that paint? (Accept reasonable responses.)
6. (After the group has completed reading the story and answering the comprehension questions, tell the students the total number of points to record in Box B of their Point Chart. Maximum = 8 points.)

INDIVIDUAL READING CHECKOUTS

═══ EXERCISE 7 ═══

READING CHECKOUTS

1. For this part of the lesson, assigned pairs of students work together during the checkouts.
2. Each student does two checkouts.
   a. First checkout: Students can earn 2 points by making no more than 2 errors on the first part of story 32. Students record points in Box C-1 of their Point Chart.
   b. Second checkout: One-minute timed reading. Students can earn 2 points by reading at least 105 words and making no more than 3 errors on the first part of story 31. Students record points in Box C-2 of their Point Chart and plot their reading rate on the Individual Reading Progress chart.

WORKBOOK EXERCISES

Independent Student Work

1. Open your Workbook to Lesson 32. ✔ Complete all parts of your workbook lesson. If you make no more than 3 errors, you earn 4 points.
2. (After checking the Workbooks, direct students who made no more than 3 errors to record 4 points in Box D of their Point Chart.)

Lesson Point Summary
Tell students to add the points in Boxes A, B, C-1, C-2, and D, plus any bonus points they have earned, and to write this number in the Total box of the Point Chart.

END OF LESSON 32

LESSON **32**

1 Write **1, 2,** or **3** in front of each sentence to show when these things happened in the story. Then write the sentences in the blanks.

____1____ Irma took a coin from her purse and dropped the coin on the paint.
____3____ Irma dropped the coin in the boiling water.
____2____ The coin became invisible.

1. Irma took a coin from her purse and dropped the coin on the paint.
2. The coin became invisible.
3. Irma dropped the coin in the boiling water.

2 Write the answers to these questions:
1. What happened to the coin when Irma hit it with a hammer? (It got flatter and bigger.)
2. How did Irma make the rag become visible again? (by soaking it in motor oil)
3. What did Berta want? (ice cream)
4. What was Irma thinking at the end of this story? (that she could have a lot of fun with the invisible paint)

3 The words in the first column have endings. Write the same words without endings in the second column.

boarder	board
eaten	eat
washing	wash
flatter	flat
waved	wave

34 LESSON 32   Copyright © SRA/McGraw-Hill

Lesson 32 from Decoding B2 TPB

1

A	B	C	D	E
food	burn	benches	pointed	load
fold	barn	beaches	painted	loud

2

soiled   cooled   eaten   watched   pounded

3

listened   tests   invisible   copper
silver   glass   flatter   visible
grime   lazy   removes   relatives
freezer   stomped   floor

4 # Irma Tests the Invisible Paint

Irma had left a nail on the hard paint. When she came back to her lab, the nail was invisible. Slowly she began to realize that the paint had made the nail invisible.

She said to herself, "I will test that paint." She took a coin from her purse and dropped the coin on the paint. Then she watched and waited. After a while, she saw that the coin was starting to turn invisible. It now looked like a glass coin. She could still see it, but it did not look like a copper coin or a silver coin. It looked like a glass <u>coin</u>.

[1]

She dropped it on the floor. "Clink," it went. It sounded like a coin. She took a hammer and hit the coin ten times. She wanted to see what would happen to it now. The coin got flatter and bigger, but it still looked like glass. She said, "I don't believe what is happening."

She set the coin on the paint again and waited. Soon the coin was invisible. Now it didn't look like glass. It didn't look like anything.

"I don't believe it," Irma said to herself. She felt the coin. She could feel the dents that had been made by the hammer.

[1]

LESSON 32 **65**

Irma closed her eyes and picked up the coin. "It feels like it should feel," she said to herself. Then she opened her eyes and looked at the coin in her hand. It was invisible.

She said, "I must see how this invisible paint works." She got a pot of water and heated it on the stove in her lab. When the water began to boil, she dropped the coin into it. Then she watched to see what would happen.

Slowly she could see the coin begin to form at the bottom of the boiling water. Slowly it became visible. At first the coin looked like glass. Then it began to look like a coin that had been pounded with a hammer.

[1]

She lifted the coin from the boiling water and set it on a sheet of foil. When the coin had cooled, she picked it up and looked at it. She said, "I know that I can remove the invisible paint with boiling water. Now I will try something else."

She took a soiled rag and tore off a small bit. She set the bit of rag on the hard paint. Then she watched as the rag became invisible.

"Now I will see if something else will remove that invisible paint." She took the bit of soiled rag and dropped it in the washtub. Then she turned on the cold water and let it run over the rag.

[2]

The water washed away bits of grime. As each bit of grime left the rag, a spot became visible. But the rest of the rag was still invisible. "Cold water does not seem to work too well," Irma said.

Then she took a can of motor oil from the shelf. She filled a cup with oil and dropped the rag into the cup of oil. Slowly the rag became visible. Irma smiled. She said, "Oil removes the invisible paint."

Now Irma had to think. She could hardly believe what had happened. She went over everything five times. Then she shook her head and said, "It must have happened. I must have made a paint that turns things invisible."

[2]

"Irma," Berta called from upstairs, "what happened to that gallon of ice cream that was in the freezer?"

Irma said, "If it's not in the freezer, you must have eaten it."

Berta yelled, "Well, why didn't you get more? How can we watch TV if we don't have ice cream?"

Irma said, "You'll just have to do the best you can."

Berta did not say anything. She stomped back to the living room. As Irma listened to her lazy boarder walking across the floor, she got an idea. She smiled and said to herself, "I think I can have a lot of fun with this invisible paint."

[1]

66 *LESSON 32*

Lesson 32 from Decoding B2 Student Book

LESSON 32

1 Write **1, 2,** or **3** in front of each sentence to show when these things happened in the story. Then write the sentences in the blanks.

_____ **Irma took a coin from her purse and dropped the coin on the paint.**

_____ **Irma dropped the coin in the boiling water.**

_____ **The coin became invisible.**

1. _____

  _____

2. _____

  _____

3. _____

  _____

2 Write the answers to these questions:

1. What happened to the coin when Irma hit it with a hammer?

  _____

2. How did Irma make the rag become visible again?

  _____

3. What did Berta want? _____

4. What was Irma thinking at the end of this story? _____

  _____

3 The words in the first column have endings. Write the same words without endings in the second column.

boarder _____

eaten _____

washing _____

flatter _____

waved _____

Lesson 32 from Decoding B2 Workbook

▶ Decoding C—Lesson 26

The vocabulary for stories 1–25 consolidates the skills presented in **Decoding B1** and **B2,** providing a review for students who completed **Decoding B2** and an introduction for new students.

New affixes **ex** and **un** are introduced (Exercises 1 and 2) in Lesson 26. Previously taught sound combinations are reviewed (Exercise 3). Vocabulary exercises present meanings for familiar words such as **tunnel** and words such as **emerged** that are probably unfamiliar to many students (Exercise 4). New informational words **(sequoia, canopy, foliage)** are included in a word list (Exercise 5).

This story is the first factual selection in **Decoding C.** The vocabulary and sentence structure are not particularly complex; however, the selection presents a great deal of information. Specified comprehension items (numbered 1 through 3) are presented after students read each section of the story (Exercise 7). If the group makes more than 12 decoding errors during the oral reading of the story, it is to read the story again either immediately or during the next lesson.

Following the reading of the story, students work together in pairs. Each student reads aloud for 2 minutes and can earn points by meeting the specified rate and accuracy criteria (120 words per minute, making no more than 5 total errors).

As the last activity of the lesson, students work independently in their Workbooks. The Workbook Exercises include ten comprehension items on story 26 (part 1), vocabulary items (part 2), and word-analysis items that require students to write affixes and the root words of multisyllabic words (part 3).

Correction Reminder
Follow these steps to correct all word-identification errors during Word-Attack Exercises.

1. The word is _____.

2. What word? (Signal.)

3. Spell _____. (Signal for each lettter.) What word? (Signal.)

4. Go back to the first word in the [row/column]. ✔ What word? (Signal.)

LESSON 26

WORD-ATTACK SKILLS

Chalkboard

━━━ EXERCISE 1 ━━━

- **AFFIX: ex**

> 1. Print on the board: **tend, cite, ample, plain, pose.**

2. For each word:
   (Point to the word.) What word? (Signal.)
3. (Add **e-x** to the beginning of each word:
   extend, excite, example, explain, expose.)
4. For each word:
   (Point to the word.) What word? (Signal.)
5. (Repeat the list until firm.)

Student Book

━━━ EXERCISE 2 ━━━

- **AFFIX: un**
1. Open your Student Book to Lesson 26. ✔

> un
>
> | **A** | **B** |
> |---|---|
> | unreal | unable |
> | unseen | unloaded |
> | unbelievable | unfortunate |
> | uncertain | |

Touch the letters **u-n** in part 1. ✔ When
those letters appear at the beginning of a
word, they usually mean **not**. What does **un**
mean? (Signal.) *Not.*
2. Touch the first word in column A. ✔ What
   word? (Signal.) *Unreal.* What does **unreal**
   mean? (Signal.) *Not real.*
3. Touch the next word. ✔ What word? (Signal.)
   Unseen. What does **unseen** mean? (Signal.)
   Not seen.
4. (Repeat step 3 for each remaining word.)
5. (Repeat the list until firm.)
6. (Repeat steps 2–5 for the words in
   column B.)

━━━ EXERCISE 3 ━━━

WORD PRACTICE

1. Touch the first word in part 2. ✔

> bright   easily   interesting   contained
> distance   gigantic   although   falter
> fifteenth   branches   approaches   flights
> matches   bloating   frightened

What sound? (Signal.) *īī.* What word?
(Signal.) *Bright.*
2. Touch the next word. ✔ What sound?
   (Signal.) *ēēē.* What word? (Signal.) *Easily.*
3. (Repeat step 2 for each remaining word.)
4. (Repeat each row of words until firm.)

━━━ EXERCISE 4 ━━━

VOCABULARY

1. Touch part 3. ✔

> 3 1. tunnel
>   2. fluttered
>   3. snaked
>   4. drizzly
>   5. emerged

We're going to talk about what those
words mean.
2. Touch word 1. ✔ What word? (Signal.)
   Tunnel. Who can tell me what a **tunnel** is?
   (Call on a student.) Idea: A passage through
   water or mountains.
3. Everybody, touch word 2. ✔ What word?
   (Signal.) *Fluttered.* **Flutter** is another way of
   saying **move back and forth rapidly**. What's
   another way of saying "The leaf **moved back
   and forth rapidly** down to the ground"?
   (Signal.) *The leaf fluttered down to the
   ground.*
4. Touch word 3. ✔ What word? (Signal.)
   Snaked. **Snaked** is another way of saying
   twisted. Everybody, what's another way of
   saying "The road **twisted** between the
   mountains"? (Signal.) *The road snaked
   between the mountains.*

5. Touch word 4. ✔ What word? (Signal.) *Drizzly.* Who knows what a **drizzly** rain is like? (Call on a student.) Idea: A light, quiet rain.

6. Everybody, touch word 5. ✔ What word? (Signal.) *Emerged.* When you **emerge** from a place, you **come out of** that place. What's another way of saying "The woman **came out of** the office"? (Signal.) *The woman emerged from the office.*

═══════ **EXERCISE 5** ═══════

WORD PRACTICE

1. Touch the first word in part 4. ✔

> **4** sequoia canopy foliage building
> swirled darkness drifted develop
> survive through swayed Pacific
> November create covered arrangements
> suggested instruments neither

What word? (Signal.) *Sequoia.*

2. Next word. ✔ What word? (Signal.) *Canopy.*
3. (Repeat step 2 for each remaining word.)
4. (Repeat each row of words until firm.)

═══════ **EXERCISE 6** ═══════

WORD-ATTACK SKILLS: Individual Test

1. (Call on individual students. Each student reads a row or column. Tally the rows and columns read without error. If the group reads at least 10 rows and columns without making errors, direct all students to record 5 points in Box A of their Point Chart.)

2. (If the group did not read at least 10 rows and columns without errors, do not award any points for the Word-Attack exercises.)

GROUP READING

═══════ **EXERCISE 7** ═══════

STORY READING

1. Everybody, touch part 5. ✔
2. The error limit for this story is twelve. If the group reads the story with twelve errors or less, you earn 5 points.
3. (Call on a student to read the story title.) What do you think this story is about?
4. (Call on individual students to each read two to four sentences.)
5. (Call on individual students to answer comprehension questions during the selection reading.)

5

THE REDWOOD TREE

This is the story of a redwood tree that is living today in Northern California. That redwood, like many others, has had an interesting life.

Its life began with a seed contained in a cone. A redwood cone is about as big as a quarter. The cone starts to grow in early summer. By late summer it is full-sized and bright green with many seeds inside. The cone is not yet full grown, however. As fall approaches, the cone begins to change color, turning brown. Small flaps on all sides of the cone open, and as they do the tiny seeds fall out. The seeds are so small that ten of them would easily fit on the end of your finger. If you wanted half a kilogram of these seeds, you would have to collect about 120 thousand of them.₁

1. How big is a redwood cone? Idea: About as big as a quarter.
1. How big are the redwood seeds? Ideas: Very small; so small that ten could fit on the end of your finger.

It seems strange that a seed so small can grow into the world's tallest tree, but it's true. Redwoods are the tallest trees, although a cousin of the redwood—the giant sequoia—has a thicker trunk than the redwood. Some giant sequoias have trunks so thick that people have constructed tunnels through them and these tunnels are so big that cars can pass through them. The giant sequoia, however, does not grow as tall as the redwood. To get an idea of how tall the bigger redwoods are, imagine what it would be like to climb a flight of stairs as high as these redwoods. Imagine climbing five flights of stairs. Imagine how far down it is when you are five stories high. A big redwood is much taller than a five-story building, however. So imagine going up to the tenth floor, the fifteenth floor, the twentieth floor. From up here you can see a long distance, and it's a long, long way down. However, if you were on the twentieth floor of a building, you would not be near the top of a big redwood. You would probably be tired from climbing twenty flights of stairs; however, to reach the top of a big redwood, you would have to climb another fifteen flights of stairs. That's right. A very tall redwood is about as tall as a thirty-five-story building. A person standing down at the base of the tree would look like an ant. The base of the redwood's trunk is so big that eight people could stand next to each other and hide behind the trunk. And that gigantic tree develops from a seed smaller than a grain of wheat.[2]

2. Which kinds of trees are the tallest? *Redwoods.*
2. Which kinds of trees have the thickest trunks? *Giant sequoias.*
2. How tall is a very tall redwood? Idea: About as tall as a 35-story building.

It was on a sunny November day that the seed of the redwood tree in this story fluttered from the cone. The parent tree stood on the bank of a small creek that snaked among the giant redwoods. The weather had been cold, and a drizzly rain had been falling for days. During the rain, the flaps of the redwood cone swelled up and closed. But now the sun emerged, and a brisk wind swirled through the tops of the redwoods, bending their tops to the south. As the top of the parent tree swayed in the cool wind, the cones began to dry out, and the flaps began to open. Below, the forest was deeply shaded by the foliage of the giant redwoods, which formed a canopy of green that extended as far as one could see. In the distance was the sound of the Pacific Ocean.

Late that afternoon, a sudden gust of wind pushed through the forest, bending branches of the redwoods. When that wind hit the parent tree, six of the cone's forty seeds fluttered down and drifted down, down, into the dark forest below. One of those seeds would develop into a giant. The others would not survive.[3]

3. When did the seeds from the redwood tree flutter from the cone? Idea: On a very sunny November day.
3. How many seeds fluttered down? *Six.*
3. How many seeds survived? *One.*
6. (Award points quickly.)
7. (If the group makes more than twelve errors, repeat the reading immediately or on the next day.)

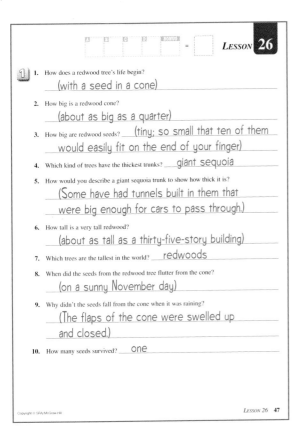

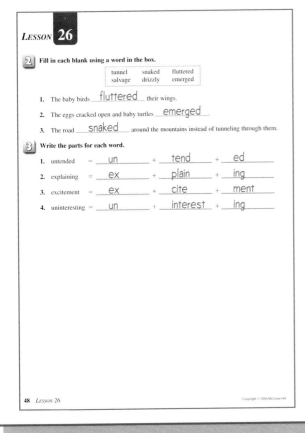

A   B   C   D   BONUS   =   [ ]   LESSON 26

① 1. How does a redwood tree's life begin?
   (with a seed in a cone)

2. How big is a redwood cone?
   (about as big as a quarter)

3. How big are redwood seeds?   (tiny; so small that ten of them
   would easily fit on the end of your finger)

4. Which kind of trees have the thickest trunks?   giant sequoia

5. How would you describe a giant sequoia trunk to show how thick it is?
   (Some have had tunnels built in them that
   were big enough for cars to pass through.)

6. How tall is a very tall redwood?
   (about as tall as a thirty-five-story building)

7. Which trees are the tallest in the world?   redwoods

8. When did the seeds from the redwood tree flutter from the cone?
   (on a sunny November day)

9. Why didn't the seeds fall from the cone when it was raining?
   (The flaps of the cone were swelled up
   and closed.)

10. How many seeds survived?   one

Copyright © SRA/McGraw-Hill   LESSON 26   47

LESSON 26

② Fill in each blank using a word in the box.

| tunnel | snaked | fluttered |
| salvage | drizzly | emerged |

1. The baby birds fluttered their wings.

2. The eggs cracked open and baby turtles emerged .

3. The road snaked around the mountains instead of tunneling through them.

③ Write the parts for each word.

1. untended   = un   + tend   + ed
2. explaining = ex   + plain + ing
3. excitement = ex   + cite   + ment
4. uninteresting = un + interest + ing

48 LESSON 26   Copyright © SRA/McGraw-Hill

INDIVIDUAL READING CHECKOUTS

EXERCISE 8

TIMED READING CHECKOUTS

1. (For this part of the lesson, assigned pairs of students work together during the checkouts.)

2. (Each student does a two-minute timed reading, starting with the first sentence of the story. Students earn 5 points by reading at least 240 words and making no more than 5 errors on the first part of story 26. Students record points in Box C of their Point Chart and plot their errors and reading rate on the Individual Reading Progress chart.)

WORKBOOK EXERCISES

Independent Student Work

Task A

Open your Workbook to Lesson 26. Complete all parts of your Workbook lesson. If you make no errors, you will earn 5 points.

Task B

1. (Before presenting Lesson 27, check student Workbooks for Lesson 26. Direct students who work in pairs for the checkouts to exchange Workbooks.)

2. (Call on individual students to read the questions and answers in part 1.)

3. (Call on individual students to read the answers to the items in parts 2 and 3.)

4. (Direct the students to count the number of errors on the Workbook checked and write the number at the top.)

5. (Award points and direct students to record their points in Box D of their Point Chart.)
   0 errors . . . . 5 points
   1 error . . . . 3 points
   2 or 3 errors. . . . . 1 point
   More than 3 errors. . . . . 0 points

END OF LESSON 26

un

A	B
unreal	unable
unseen	unloaded
unbelievable	unfortunate
uncertain	

---

bright   easily   interesting   contained
distance   gigantic   although   falter
fifteenth   branches   approaches   flights
matches   bloating   frightened

---

1. tunnel
2. fluttered
3. snaked
4. drizzly
5. emerged

---

sequoia   canopy   foliage   building
swirled   darkness   drifted   develop
survive   through   swayed   Pacific
November   create   covered   arrangements
suggested   instruments   neither

The Redwood Tree

This is the story of a redwood tree that is living today in Northern California. That redwood, like many others, has had an interesting life.

Its life began with a seed contained in a cone. A redwood cone is about as big as a quarter. The cone starts to grow in early summer. By late summer it is full-sized and bright green with many seeds inside. The cone is not yet full grown, however. As fall approaches, the cone begins to change color, turning brown. Small flaps on all sides of the cone open, and as they do the * tiny seeds fall out. The seeds are so small that ten of them would easily fit on the end of your finger. If you wanted half a kilogram of these seeds, you would have to collect about 120 thousand of them.₁

It seems strange that a seed so small can grow into the world's tallest tree, but it's true. Redwoods are the tallest trees, although a cousin of the redwood—the giant sequoia—has a thicker trunk than the redwood. Some giant sequoias have trunks so thick that people have constructed tunnels through them and these tunnels are so big * that cars can pass through them. The giant sequoia, however, does not grow as tall as the redwood. To get an idea of how tall the bigger redwoods are, imagine what it would be like to climb a flight of stairs as high as these redwoods. Imagine climbing five flights of stairs. Imagine how far down it is when you are five stories high. A big redwood is much taller than a five-story building, however. So imagine going up to the tenth floor, the fifteenth floor, the twentieth floor. From up here you can see a long distance, and * it's a long, long way down. However, if you were on the twentieth floor of a building, you would not be near the top of a big redwood. You would probably be tired from climbing twenty flights of stairs; however, to reach the top of a big redwood, you would have to climb another fifteen flights of stairs. That's right. A very tall redwood is about as tall as a thirty-five-story building. A person standing down at the base of the tree would look like an ant. The base of the redwood's trunk is so big that eight * people could stand next to each other and hide behind the trunk. And that gigantic tree develops from a seed smaller than a grain of wheat.₂

It was on a sunny November day that the seed of the redwood tree in this story fluttered from the cone. The parent tree stood on the bank of a small creek that snaked among the giant redwoods. The weather had been cold, and a drizzly rain had been falling for days. During the rain, the flaps of the redwood cone swelled up and closed. But now the sun emerged, and a brisk wind * swirled through the tops of the redwoods, bending their tops to the south. As the top of the parent tree swayed in the cool wind, the cones began to dry out, and the flaps began to open. Below, the forest was deeply shaded by the foliage of the giant redwoods, which formed a canopy of green that extended as far as one could see. In the distance was the sound of the Pacific Ocean.

Late that afternoon, a sudden gust of wind pushed through the forest, bending branches of the redwoods. When that wind hit the parent tree, six of * the cone's forty seeds fluttered down and drifted down, down, into the dark forest below. One of those seeds would develop into a giant. The others would not survive.₃

Lesson 26 from Decoding C Student Book

1. 1. How does a redwood tree's life begin?

_____

2. How big is a redwood cone?

_____

3. How big are redwood seeds? _____

_____

4. Which kind of trees have the thickest trunks? _____

5. How would you describe a giant sequoia trunk to show how thick it is?

_____

_____

6. How tall is a very tall redwood?

_____

7. Which trees are the tallest in the world? _____

8. When did the seeds from the redwood tree flutter from the cone?

_____

9. Why didn't the seeds fall from the cone when it was raining?

_____

_____

10. How many seeds survived? _____

LESSON 26

2 Fill in each blank using a word in the box.

tunnel	snaked	fluttered
salvage	drizzly	emerged

1. The baby birds _____ their wings.

2. The eggs cracked open and baby turtles _____.

3. The road _____ around the mountains instead of tunneling through them.

3 Write the parts for each word.

1. untended = _____ + _____ + _____

2. explaining = _____ + _____ + _____

3. excitement = _____ + _____ + _____

4. uninteresting = _____ + _____ + _____

▶ Decoding C—Lesson 118

By Lesson 118, students have learned 11 affixes. The word-attack portion of the lesson is shorter. The meanings of the affixes **sub, able, dis, re,** and **ly** are reviewed (Exercise 2). Word parts are reviewed (Exercise 3). Fairly sophisticated words are presented (Exercise 4), and vocabulary words are presented (Exercise 5).

The reading selection is longer than the redwood selection in Lesson 26. The writing style is similar to typical text material, using complex sentences and conveying a great deal of information.

After the group reading of the story, students read a 300- to 400-word passage taken from an outside source. Before reading this passage, they do a brief word-attack list (Exercise 8, task A).

Following the passage reading, students work in pairs doing a 2-minute oral reading of story 118 (reading a minimum of 130 words per minute with no more than 5 total errors).

As homework, students write answers to the comprehension items and vocabulary items presented in the Workbook. Answers are checked at the beginning of the next class period.

LESSON 118

WORKBOOK EXERCISES

Workcheck

━━━━━━━━━━ EXERCISE 1 ━━━━━━━━━━

CHECKING HOMEWORK

1. (Direct students who work in pairs for the checkouts to exchange Workbooks and to open the Workbooks to Lesson 117.)
2. (Call on individual students to read the questions and answers in part 1.)
3. (Call on individual students to read the answers to the items in part 2.)
4. (Direct the students to count the number of errors on the Workbook checked and write the number at the top.)
5. (Award points and direct students to record their points in Box D of their Point Chart.)

0 errors	5 points
1 error	3 points
2 or 3 errors.	1 point
More than 3 errors.	0 points

LESSON 117

1. 1. Name the three types of doctors who worked in 1500.
   a. surgeons of the long robe
   b. physicians
   c. barber-surgeons

2. Why did surgeons of the long robe "bleed" patients?
   (They thought it would help patients recover from diseases caused by sluggish blood.)

3. What kind of work did physicians do?
   (lectured at universities and gave advice to people who could afford to hire them)

4. What language did physicians and surgeons speak and read? Latin

5. What kind of work was done in a "barber shop"?
   (cutting hair; amputations; lancing boils; teeth pulling; removing bullets)

6. Why was it a crime for doctors to study dead bodies?
   (People believed that a person would not reach heaven if the body was cut into pieces.)

7. What does *anatomy* mean?
   (the structure of the body)

LESSON 117

8. a. How did doctors study anatomy?
   (by operating on animals)

   b. Why didn't this method help to find out facts about the human body?
   (The human body is not the same as an animal's body.)

9. What did Leonardo and Paré seek? (the facts)

2. Fill in each blank using a word in the box.

wounds	amputate	sluggish
purify	ignorant	scalding

1. You are ignorant of something that you do not know.
2. Barb felt slow and sluggish in the mornings.
3. After I purify the water, the germs will all be dead.

Lesson 118 from Decoding C TPB C2

WORD-ATTACK SKILLS

Student Book

===== EXERCISE 2 =====

AFFIX REVIEW

1. Open your Student Book to Lesson 118. ✔

 sub   able   dis   re   ly

Touch part 1. ✔ Let's see if you remember a meaning for each of those affixes.

2. Touch the letters **s-u-b.** ✔ (Call on a student.) What's one meaning of **sub?** Accept **under** or **less than.** (Call on another student.) What's another meaning of **sub?**

3. Everybody, touch the letters **a-b-l-e.** ✔ What's one meaning of **able?** (Signal.) *Able to be.*

4. Touch the letters **d-i-s.** ✔ (Call on a student.) What's one meaning of **dis?** Accept **not, the opposite of,** or **away from.** (Call on another student.) What's another meaning of **dis?**

5. Everybody, touch the letters **r-e.** ✔ What's one meaning of **re?** (Signal.) *Again.*

6. Touch the letters **l-y.** ✔ What's one meaning of **ly?** (Signal.) *How something happened.*

===== EXERCISE 3 =====

WORD PRACTICE

1. Touch the first word in part 2. ✔

2 special   substance   extract*   deserve*

What's the underlined part? (Signal.) *shull.* What word? (Signal.) *Special.*

2. Touch the next word. ✔ What's the underlined part? (Signal.) *sub.* What word? (Signal.) *Substance.*

3. (Repeat step 2 for each remaining word.)

4. (Repeat the row of words until firm.)

5. What does **extract** mean? (Call on a student. Repeat for **deserve.**)

===== EXERCISE 4 =====

WORD PRACTICE

1. Touch the first word in part 3. ✔

 3 treatments   submarine   eventually   devices*   conditions   filthy   corpses   dissected   sponge   warfare   anatomist   patients   completed   battlefield   muscles   statues   amputate

What word? (Signal.) *Treatments.*

2. Next word. ✔ What word? (Signal.) *Submarine.*

3. (Repeat step 2 for each remaining word.)

4. (Repeat each row of words until firm.)

5. What does **devices** mean? (Call on a student.)

===== EXERCISE 5 =====

VOCABULARY

1. Touch part 4. ✔

4
1. selection
2. sketches
3. masterpieces
4. anatomy
5. dressings
6. limbs

We're going to talk about what those words mean.

2. Touch word 1. ✔ What word? (Signal.) *Selection.* A **selection** is **a portion of something.** Everybody, what do we call **a portion of something?** (Signal.) *A selection.*

3. Touch word 2. ✔ What word? (Signal.) *Sketches.* (Call on a student.) What are **sketches?** Idea: Rough, quick drawings.

4. Everybody, touch word 3. ✔ What word? (Signal.) *Masterpieces.* **Masterpieces** are **fine works of art.** Everybody, what's another way of saying "The painting was a fine work of art"? (Signal.) *The painting was a masterpiece.*

5. Touch word 4. ✔ What word? (Signal.) *Anatomy.* **Anatomy** is **the study of the body.** Everybody, what is **the study of the body** called? (Signal.) *Anatomy.*

6. Touch word 5. ✔ What word? (Signal.) *Dressings.* **Bandages that cover a wound** are called **dressings.** Everybody, what do we call **bandages that cover a wound?** (Signal.) *Dressings.*

7. Touch word 6. ✔ What word? (Signal.) *Limbs.* Arms and legs are **limbs.** Everybody, what are arms and legs? (Signal.) *Limbs.*

═══════ **EXERCISE 6** ═══════

WORD-ATTACK SKILLS: Individual Test
(Call on individual students. Each student reads a row or column.)

SELECTION READING

═══════ **EXERCISE 7** ═══════

STORY READING

1. Everybody, touch part 5. ✔
2. The error limit for this story is twelve. If the group reads the story with twelve errors or less, you earn 5 points.
3. (Call on a student to read the story title.) What do you think this story is about?
4. (Call on individual students to each read two to four sentences.)
5. (Call on individual students to answer comprehension questions during the story reading.)

THE EARLY STUDY OF ANATOMY AND SURGERY

After you read this selection, look up some of the paintings of Leonardo da Vinci. When you examine these paintings, look at the way Leonardo drew the human body. Leonardo understood the structure of the human body probably as well as anybody who had ever lived. And he reached this understanding of the body by studying its inner structure. He worked with corpses (dead bodies), and he dissected them (cut parts away so that he could study other parts). He recorded his findings by making sketches of the body parts. He made detailed drawings of muscles, bones, even nerves. He hoped to publish a great work on the anatomy of the human body. Unfortunately, he died before he completed the book. All that he left behind were hundreds of notes and sketches. Many of these were lost after his death, but some were saved. These notes and sketches found their way to different parts of Europe.[1]

1. How did Leonardo learn so much about human anatomy? Idea: By dissecting and studying human corpses.
1. What had he hoped to publish? Idea: A great work on human anatomy.

Leonardo also left sketches of another kind. Among them were details for building a submarine, an airplane, and other devices that would not be "invented" for hundreds of years. Besides the devices that remained on paper, he did invent machines that were actually used to construct buildings, make statues, and create special effects for plays. He created paintings that are considered masterpieces. He helped open the door to the study of human anatomy. But he never saw some of his greatest achievements accepted by the world.[2]

2. What were some of Leonardo's accomplishments? **Ideas:** He drew plans for building a submarine, an airplane, and other inventions; he built machines that were used in construction; he painted masterpieces.

2. Why might Leonardo have felt like a failure? **Idea:** Because he never saw some of his greatest achievements accepted by the world.

A very different kind of contribution to medicine in the 1500s was made by a man called Ambroise Paré. Paré was not an anatomist or an artist. He began as a helper to a barber-surgeon in a hospital of more than one thousand beds. Conditions in that hospital were terrible even by the standards of that time. Rats could be seen in every part of the building. The bedding and the dressings of the wounds were filthy. The odor was so bad that the attendants could not enter the sickroom unless they held a sponge dipped in vinegar over their nose and mouth. The patients were not fed regularly.3

3. How did Paré begin his work in medicine? **Idea:** As a helper to a barber-surgeon in a hospital.

3. What were the conditions in the hospital in which Paré worked? **Ideas:** Terrible; there were rats; it was filthy; it smelled awful.

After three years of working in the hospital, Paré became an army surgeon. Conditions for treating soldiers on the battlefield were as bad as those in the hospital. The surgeons would amputate limbs or try to extract bullets from gunshot wounds. Bullets were new in warfare, and the surgeons did not know how to treat the wounds bullets caused. Some cut out the bullet and then poured hot oil into the wound. These surgeons used the slogan: "If the wound is not curable by using the knife, use fire." (*Fire* meant hot oil.)4

4. Where did Paré work after he left the hospital? **Idea:** In the army.

4. How did surgeons treat bullet wounds? **Idea:** By cutting out the bullet and pouring hot oil into the wound.

Paré changed two things. First, he discovered how to tie off arteries in amputations so that the patient did not bleed to death. Second, he discovered that wounds healed better without boiling oil. Instead, he used clean cloth and mild substances like egg whites to cover the wounds. Paré's methods worked. Many of the soldiers that Paré treated lived. Many didn't suffer as much as if they had received the usual treatments. They usually didn't develop fevers, and the wounds healed more quickly.5

5. Name the two changes Paré made in treating wounds. **Ideas:** He tied off arteries in amputations and he didn't treat wounds with boiling oil.

People began to become aware of the work of Paré. He became court surgeon to three kings. In his day, many other doctors thought surgery was below their dignity. Paré helped raise the standing of surgery. But many physicians and surgeons resented Paré. They didn't believe in his methods. They thought he was an ignorant man because he didn't even know Latin.

Paré did a lot of things to advance medicine. He developed new methods for delivering babies and cut down the number of deaths among mothers and newborn babies. The methods that Paré developed were eventually adopted by others. In fact, when he died, his methods were being used in the hospital where he had begun as a barber's assistant.6

6. Why didn't other doctors respect Paré? **Ideas:** They thought he was ignorant because he didn't speak Latin; they didn't believe in his methods.

6. What did Paré do to help women? **Ideas:** He developed new methods for delivering babies; he cut down on the number of deaths among mothers and newborn babies.

6. (Award points quickly.)

7. (If the group makes more than twelve errors, repeat the reading immediately or on the next day.)

EXERCISE 8

INFORMATION-PASSAGE READING

Task A Word-Attack Practice

1. (Present the passage you have selected.) I can write as many as fifteen words on the board. Study the story for one minute and ask about any words you don't know.

2. Print only the words the students ask about. (Put no more than fifteen words on the board.)

3. For each word:
   (Point to the word. Pause.) What word? (Signal.)

4. (Briefly discuss the meanings of unfamiliar words. Use each unfamiliar word in a sentence.)

5. (Do not spend more than five minutes on this word-attack practice.)

Task B Group Reading

1. The error limit for this information passage is eight. If the group reads the passage with eight errors or less, you earn 5 points.

2. (If there is a title, call on a student to read the title.) What is this passage about?

3. (Call on individual students to each read two to four sentences.)

4. (Ask some comprehension questions during the reading of the passage.)

5. (At the end of the reading ask:) What is the main idea of this passage? (or) What are the main points of this passage? (Call on several students.)

6. (If the group reads the passage with no more than eight errors, tell the students to record 5 points in Box B of the Point Chart. If the group makes more than eight errors, tell the students to record 0 points in Box B.)

EXERCISE 9

TIMED READING CHECKOUTS

1. (For this part of the lesson, assigned pairs of students work together during the checkouts.)

2. (Each student does a two-minute timed reading, starting with the first sentence of the story. Students earn 5 points by reading at least 260 words and making no more than 5 errors on the first part of story 118. Students record points in Box C of their Point Chart and plot their errors and reading rate on the Individual Reading Progress chart.)

WORKBOOK EXERCISES

Assignment

Before the next lesson, complete Workbook Lesson 118. If you make no errors, you will earn 5 points.

END OF LESSON 118

1 sub able dis re ly

2 special substance extract deserve

3 treatments submarine eventually
devices conditions filthy corpses
dissected sponge warfare anatomist
patients completed battlefield
muscles statues amputate

4
1. selection
2. sketches
3. masterpieces
4. anatomy
5. dressings
6. limbs

5 # The Early Study of Anatomy and Surgery

After you read this selection, look up some of the paintings of Leonardo da Vinci. When you examine these paintings, look at the way Leonardo drew the human body. Leonardo understood the structure of the human body probably as well as anybody who had ever lived. And he reached this understanding of the body by studying its inner structure. He worked with corpses (dead bodies), and he dissected them (cut parts away so that he could study other parts). He recorded his findings by making sketches of the body parts. He made detailed drawings of muscles, bones, even nerves. He * hoped to publish a great work on the anatomy of the human body. Unfortunately, he died before he completed the book. All that he left behind were hundreds of notes and sketches. Many of these were lost after his death, but some were saved. These notes and sketches found their way to different parts of Europe.1

LESSON 118 **245**

Leonardo also left sketches for another kind. Among them were details for building a submarine, an airplane, and other devices that would not be "invented" for hundreds of years. Besides the devices that remained on paper, he did invent machines that were actually used * to construct buildings, make statues, and create special effects for plays. He created paintings that are considered masterpieces. He helped open the door to the study of human anatomy. But he never saw some of his greatest achievements accepted by the world.[2]

A very different kind of contribution to medicine in the 1500s was made by a man called <u>Ambroise</u> Paré. Paré was not an anatomist or an artist. He began as a helper to a barber-surgeon in a hospital of more than one thousand beds. Conditions in that hospital were terrible even by the standards of that time. * Rats could be seen in every part of the building. The bedding and the dressings of the wounds were filthy. The odor was so bad that the attendants could not enter the sickroom unless they held a sponge dipped in vinegar over their nose and mouth. The patients were not fed regularly.[3]

After three years of working in the hospital, Paré became an army surgeon. Conditions for treating soldiers on the battlefield were as bad as those in the hospital. The surgeons would amputate limbs or try to extract bullets from gunshot wounds. Bullets were new in warfare, and the * surgeons did not know how to treat the wounds bullets caused. Some cut out the bullet and then poured hot oil into the wound.

These surgeons used the slogan: "If the wound is not curable by using the knife, use fire." (*Fire* meant hot oil.)[4]

Paré changed two things. First, he discovered how to tie off arteries in amputations so that the patient did not bleed to death. Second, he discovered that wounds healed better without boiling oil. Instead, he used clean cloth and mild substances like egg whites to cover the wounds. Paré's methods worked. Many of the soldiers * that Paré treated lived. Many didn't suffer as much as if they had received the usual treatments. They usually didn't develop fevers, and the wounds healed more quickly.[5]

People began to become aware of the work of Paré. He became court surgeon to three kings. In his day, many other doctors thought surgery was below their dignity. Paré helped raise the standing of surgery. But many physicians and surgeons resented Paré. They didn't believe in his methods. They thought he was an ignorant man because he didn't even know Latin.

Paré did a lot of things to advance medicine. He * developed new methods for delivering babies and cut down the number of deaths among mothers and newborn babies. The methods that Paré developed were eventually adopted by others. In fact, when he died, his methods were being used in the hospital where he had begun as a barber's assistant.[6]

246   *LESSON 118*

A   B   C   D   =

1. 1. How did Leonardo learn so much about human anatomy?

_____

2. What had Leonardo hoped to publish?

_____

3. Name two other things that Leonardo accomplished.

_____

_____

_____

4. How did Paré begin his work in medicine?

_____

5. What were the two things that battlefield surgeons could do for wounded soldiers?

_____

6. What slogan did army surgeons use when treating wounds?

_____

_____

7. What two changes did Paré make in treating wounds?

a. _____

_____

b. _____

_____

8. How did these two changes help wounded soldiers?

_____

_____

Lesson 118 from Decoding C Workbook

9. Why did many doctors not respect Paré?

_____

_____

_____

10. What did Paré do to help women?

_____

_____

_____

2 | **Fill in each blank using a word in the box.**

sketches	selection	ignorant
dressing	anatomy	masterpiece

1. The artist drew quick _____ of the model.

2. She wrapped his wound in a clean _____.

3. A class in _____ studies the human body.

Comprehension A— Lesson 12

The following core skills that will later be incorporated in more sophisticated applications are introduced and reviewed in this lesson.

▲ Deductions involving **all** and **every, no** and **don't** (Exercises 1–3)

▲ Review of how objects are the same (Exercise 4)

▲ An information game in which clues are provided for identifying an object (Exercises 5 and 6)

▲ Statement inferences (Exercise 7)

▲ Definitions and substituting new words for familiar ones in specified sentences (Exercise 8)

▲ Review of previously taught definitions (Exercise 9)

The Workbook includes the following activities.

▇ True–False (Exercises 10 and 13)

▇ Classification (Exercise 11)

▇ Same (Exercise 12)

▇ Identifying an object from a description of the object (Exercise 14)

The final part of the lesson deals with information—seasons of the year, a poem, and facts about animal classification.

Correction Reminder

Follow these steps to correct errors.

1. (Say the answer.)

2. (Repeat the task [the instructions or wording of the question].)

3. (Back up in the exercise and present the steps in order.)

4. (Finish the remaining steps in the exercise.)

5. (Repeat the entire exercise if students made more than one or two mistakes.)

THINKING OPERATIONS

═══ EXERCISE 1 ═══

DEDUCTIONS: With *all* and *every*

The first Thinking Operation today is **Deductions.**

1. I'll say rules with **all** or **every.** You say them the other way. What two words are we going to use? (Hold up one finger.) *All.* (Hold up two fingers.) *Every.*

2. Listen. **All** people learn. Say that. (Signal.) *All people learn.*
   Now say it the other way. Get ready. (Signal.) *Every person learns.*
   (Repeat step 2 until firm.)

3. Here's a new rule. **Every** person eats. Say that. (Signal.) *Every person eats.*
   Now say it the other way. Get ready. (Signal.) *All people eat.*
   (Repeat step 3 until firm.)

4. Here's a new rule. **Every** year is fifty-two weeks long. Say that. (Signal.) *Every year is fifty-two weeks long.*
   Now say it the other way. (Signal.) *All years are fifty-two weeks long.*
   (Repeat step 4 until firm.)

5. Here's a new rule. **All** objects take up space. Say that. (Signal.) *All objects take up space.*
   Now say it the other way. (Signal.) *Every object takes up space.*
   (Repeat step 5 until firm.)

═══ EXERCISE 2 ═══

DEDUCTIONS: With *no* and *don't*

Task A

1. I'll say a rule one way with the word **no.** Then I'll say it another way with the word **don't.**

2. Listen. Babies **don't** read. Say that. (Signal.) *Babies don't read.*
   Now I'll say the same rule with **no. No** babies read. Say that. (Signal.) *No babies read.*

Task B

1. Here's a new rule. **No** trucks grow. Say that. (Signal.) *No trucks grow.*

Now I'll say the same rule with **don't.** Trucks **don't** grow. Say that. (Signal.) *Trucks don't grow.*

2. Now say the rule that starts with **no trucks.** (Pause.) Get ready. (Signal.) *No trucks grow.*
   Now say the rule that starts with **trucks.** (Pause.) Get ready. (Signal.) *Trucks don't grow.* (Repeat step 2 until firm.)

Task C

1. Here's a new rule. **No** chairs eat. Say that. (Signal.) *No chairs eat.*
   Now say the rule that starts with **chairs.** (Pause.) Get ready. (Signal.) *Chairs don't eat.*
   Now say the rule that starts with **no chairs.** (Pause.) Get ready. (Signal.) *No chairs eat.* (Repeat step 1 until firm.)

2. Here's a new rule. Trees **don't** read. Say that. (Signal.) *Trees don't read.*
   Now say the rule that starts with **no trees.** (Pause.) Get ready. (Signal.) *No trees read.*
   Now say the rule that starts with **trees.** (Pause.) Get ready. (Signal.) *Trees don't read.* (Repeat step 2 until firm.)

Individual test
Call on individuals to do one step in Task C.

═══ EXERCISE 3 ═══

● **DEDUCTIONS: With *don't***

1. Listen to this rule. Dogs **don't** have wings. Everybody, say that. (Signal.) *Dogs don't have wings.*

2. Retrievers are dogs. So (pause; signal), *retrievers don't have wings.* How do you know that retrievers don't have wings? (Signal.) *Because dogs don't have wings.*

3. Listen. Dogs **don't** have wings. Beagles are dogs. So (pause; signal), *beagles don't have wings.* How do you know that beagles don't have wings? (Signal.) *Because dogs don't have wings.*

4. Listen. Dogs **don't** have wings. Poodles are dogs. So (pause; signal), *poodles don't have wings.* How do you know that poodles don't have wings? (Signal.) *Because dogs don't have wings.*

5. (Repeat steps 2–4 until firm.)

EXERCISE 14

- **DESCRIPTION**
1. Everybody, touch part E in the Workbook. ✔ Figure out which woman I describe.
2. Item 1. This woman is smiling. This woman has black hair. This woman is wearing glasses. Listen again. (Repeat the description.) Write the letter for item 1.
3. Item 2. This woman is smiling. This woman is not wearing glasses. This woman has light hair. Listen again. (Repeat the description.) Write the letter for item 2. *A.*
4. Item 3. This woman has black hair. This woman is wearing glasses. This woman is wearing earrings. Listen again. (Repeat the description.) Write the letter for item 3. *D.*
5. Let's check your answers. Mark any items you missed with an X.
6. Item 1. This woman is smiling. This woman has black hair. This woman is wearing glasses. Everybody, what letter? (Signal.) *D.*
7. (Repeat step 6 for items 2 and 3.)

Points
(Award points for Workbooks.)

INFORMATION

We're going to work on Information now.

EXERCISE 15

CALENDAR: Seasons in a Year
1. There are four seasons in a year. How many seasons are in a year? (Signal.) *Four.*
   Tell me the fact about how many seasons are in a year. (Signal.) *There are four seasons in a year.*
2. My turn to name the seasons in a year. Winter, spring, summer, fall. Your turn. Name the seasons in a year. (Signal.) *Winter, spring, summer, fall.* (Repeat until firm.)
3. You named the four (pause; signal) *seasons in a year.*
4. How many seasons are in a year? (Signal.) *Four.*

Individual test
(Call on individual students to do one of the following tasks:)
  a. Tell me the fact about how many seasons are in a year.
  b. Name the seasons in a year.

EXERCISE 16

MEMORIZATION: Poem
Task A
1. What does a mechanic do? (Call on a student. Accept reasonable responses.) Yes, a mechanic fixes cars.
2. What does an astronomer do? (Call on a student. Accept reasonable responses.) Yes, an astronomer looks at stars.
3. Who knows how you would recognize a captain in the army? (Call on a student. Accept reasonable responses.) Yes, a captain has two bars on each shoulder.
4. Who knows what sparring is? (Call on a student. Accept reasonable responses.) Yes, sparring is light boxing. Boxers spar a lot when they are getting in shape for a fight.

Task B

1. Here's a poem that tells about the things we've talked about. Listen.

   A mechanic fixes cars,
   An astronomer looks at stars,
   A captain has two bars,
   And a boxer spars and spars.

2. Let's learn that poem. Listen. A mechanic fixes cars. Say it with me. (Signal. Respond with the students. Repeat until firm.) *A mechanic fixes cars.* Your turn. (Signal.) *A mechanic fixes cars.* (Repeat until firm.)

3. An astronomer looks at stars. Say it with me. (Signal. Respond with the students.) *An astronomer looks at stars.* Your turn. (Signal.) *An astronomer looks at stars.* (Repeat until firm.)

4. A mechanic fixes cars, an astronomer looks at stars. Say it with me. (Signal. Respond with the students.) *A mechanic fixes cars, an astronomer looks at stars.* (Repeat until the students are responding with you.) Your turn. (Signal.) *A mechanic fixes cars, an astronomer looks at stars.* (Repeat until firm.)

5. A captain has two bars. Say it. (Signal.) *A captain has two bars.* (Repeat until firm.)

6. A mechanic fixes cars, an astronomer looks at stars, a captain has two bars. Say it with me. (Signal. Respond with the students.) *A mechanic fixes cars, an astronomer looks at stars, a captain has two bars.* (Repeat until students are responding with you.)
   Your turn. (Signal.) *A mechanic fixes cars, an astronomer looks at stars, a captain has two bars.* (Repeat until firm.)

7. And a boxer spars and spars. Say it. (Signal.) *And a boxer spars and spars.* (Repeat until firm.)

8. Here's the whole poem.

   A mechanic fixes cars,
   An astronomer looks at stars,
   A captain has two bars,
   And a boxer spars and spars.

   Say it with me. (Signal. Respond with the students. Repeat until students respond with you.)

9. All by yourselves. Say the poem. (Signal.) The students say the poem. (Repeat until firm.)

═══ **EXERCISE 17** ═══

INFORMATION: Animals

1. You're learning about animals that have a backbone. How many classes of those animals are there? (Signal.) *Five.*
   You've learned facts about three of those classes. Which classes? (Signal.) *Mammals, reptiles, and birds.* (Repeat until firm.)

2. The last class that you learned about was birds. Name a bird. (Call on individual students. The group is to name at least five birds.)
   You learned two facts about **all birds.** Everybody, tell me those two facts. (Hold up one finger.) First fact. *All birds have feathers.* (Hold up two fingers.) Second fact. *All birds are warm-blooded.* (Repeat until the students say the facts in order.)

3. Name a mammal. (Call on individual students. The group is to name at least five mammals.)
   You learned two facts about **all mammals.** Everybody, tell me those two facts. (Hold up one finger.) First fact. *All mammals have hair.* (Hold up two fingers.) Second fact. *All mammals are warm-blooded.* (Repeat until the students say the facts in order.)

4. Name a reptile. (Call on individual students.) The group is to name at least four reptiles.
   You learned two facts about all reptiles. Everybody, tell me those two facts. (Hold up one finger.) First fact. *All reptiles are cold-blooded.*
   (Hold up two fingers.) Second fact. *All reptiles are born on land.* (Repeat until the students say the facts in order.)

5. Tell me what class **turtles** are in. (Pause.) Get ready. (Signal.) *Reptiles.*
   So, tell me the two facts you know about turtles. (Hold up one finger.) First fact. *Turtles are cold-blooded.*
   (Hold up two fingers.) Second fact. *Turtles are born on land.* (Repeat until the students say the facts in order.)

6. Tell me what class **dogs** are in. (Pause.) Get ready. (Signal.) *Mammals.* So, tell me the two facts you know about dogs.
   (Hold up one finger.) First fact. *Dogs have hair.* (Hold up two fingers.) Second fact. *Dogs are warm-blooded.* (Repeat until the students say the facts in order.)

7. Tell me what class **hawks** are in. (Pause.) Get ready. (Signal.) *Birds.*
   So, tell me the two facts you know about hawks.
   (Hold up one finger.) First fact. *Hawks have feathers.*
   (Hold up two fingers.) Second fact. *Hawks are warm-blooded.* (Repeat until the students say the facts in order.)

Individual test
Call on individual students to do step 5, 6, or 7.

Points
(Award points for Information.
Have the students add up their daily total.)

END OF LESSON 12

1	2	3	4		TOTAL	

LESSON 12

A

1. true	false	maybe
2. true	false	maybe
3. true	false	maybe
4. true	false	maybe

B

Underline the furniture.
Make a box around the containers.

C

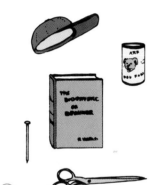

①

②

③

D

©	ⓓ	ⓔ

1. _____
2. _____
3. _____
4. _____

E

ⓐ   ⓑ   ⓒ   ⓓ

1. _____
2. _____
3. _____

LESSON 12 **23**

● Comprehension A—Lesson 52

More-sophisticated variations of the skills that were introduced earlier appear in Lesson 52. The following thinking operations are included.

▲ Statement inference involving a fairly complex sentence (Exercise 1)

▲ Deductions in which students are tested on the limitations of information conveyed by a rule (Exercise 2)

▲ Constructing deductions (Exercise 3)

▲ Definitions with new and review words—**construct, majority, inquire, consume** (Exercises 4 and 5)

▲ The use of basic evidence to explain different outcomes (Exercise 6)

▲ Review of same, opposites (Exercises 7–10)

▲ Analyzing analogies based on synonyms, opposites, and classes (Exercises 11–13)

▲ Inductions (Exercise 14)

The Workbook includes these activities.

■ Drawing deductions (Exercise 15)

■ Classifying things as objects, actions, or adjectives (Exercise 16)

■ Analogies based on information about holidays (Exercise 17)

■ Descriptions (Exercise 18)

The Information activities deal with the review of two poems.

LESSON 52

THINKING OPERATIONS

EXERCISE 1

STATEMENT INFERENCE

The first Thinking Operation today is **Statement Inference.**

1. Listen. Pollution in the air increases every year. Say that statement. (Signal.) *Pollution in the air increases every year.* (Repeat until firm.)

> **Individual test**
> Call on individuals to say the statement.

2. Everybody, listen. Pollution in the air increases every year. When does pollution increase in the air? (Signal.) *Every year.* What increases in the air every year? (Signal.) *Pollution.* Where does pollution increase every year? (Signal.) *In the air.* How does pollution in the air increase every year? (Signal.) *I don't know.* What does pollution in the air do every year? (Signal.) *Increases.* Does the pollution in the air get greater every year? (Signal.) *Yes.* (Repeat step 2 until firm.)

> **Individual test**
> Call on individual students to answer a question from step 2.

EXERCISE 2

DEDUCTIONS: With *no*

The next Thinking Operation is **Deductions.**

1. Listen to this rule. No amphibians are warm-blooded. Say the rule. (Signal.) *No amphibians are warm-blooded.*
2. **Henrietta** had a scary dream. What does the rule let you know about Henrietta? (Signal.) *Nothing.*
3. Listen. No amphibians are warm-blooded. A salamander is an **amphibian.** What does the rule let you know about a salamander?

(Signal.) *A salamander isn't warm-blooded.* How do you know that a salamander isn't warm-blooded? (Signal.) *Because no amphibians are warm-blooded.*

4. Listen. No amphibians are warm-blooded. A frog is an **amphibian.** What does the rule let you know about a frog? (Signal.) *A frog isn't warm-blooded.* How do you know that a frog isn't warm-blooded? (Signal.) *Because no amphibians are warm-blooded.*
5. Listen. No amphibians are warm-blooded. **Bill** looked for a tiger. What does the rule let you know about Bill? (Signal.) *Nothing.*
6. (Repeat steps 2–5 until firm.)

EXERCISE 3

DEDUCTIONS

1. Get ready to make a deduction.
2. Listen. Some planets have many moons. Saturn is a planet. So (pause; signal), *maybe Saturn has many moons.* (Repeat step 2 until firm.)
3. My turn to say the whole deduction. Some planets have many moons. Saturn is a planet. So, maybe Saturn has many moons.
4. Your turn. Say the whole deduction. (Signal.) *Some planets have many moons. Saturn is a planet. So, maybe Saturn has many moons.* (Repeat until firm.)

> **Individual test**
> Call on individuals to say the whole deduction.

EXERCISE 4

DEFINITIONS

The next Thinking Operation is **Definitions.**

1. **Construct** means **to make** or **to build.** What word means **to make** or **to build?** (Signal.) *Construct.*
2. Listen. He will build his house on a hill. Say that. (Signal.) *He will build his house on a hill.* (Repeat until firm.) Now say that sentence with a different word for **build.** (Pause.) Get ready. (Signal.) *He will construct his house on a hill.* (Repeat until firm.) (Repeat step 2 until firm.)

3. Listen. That building is made of concrete. Say that. (Signal.) *That building is made of concrete.* (Repeat until firm.) Now say that sentence with a different word for **made.** (Pause.) Get ready. (Signal.) *That building is constructed of concrete.* (Repeat until firm.) (Repeat step 3 until firm.)

4. Listen. She will build her own furniture. Say that. (Signal.) *She will build her own furniture.* (Repeat until firm.) Now say that with a different word for **build.** (Pause.) Get ready. (Signal.) *She will construct her own furniture.* (Repeat until firm.) (Repeat step 4 until firm.)

======== EXERCISE 5 ========

DEFINITIONS

1. **Majority.** (Pause.) What does **majority** mean? (Signal.) *More than half.* What word means **more than half?** (Signal.) *Majority.* (Repeat step 1 until firm.)

2. Listen. The **majority** of the class voted for Joyce. Say that. (Signal.) *The majority of the class voted for Joyce.* (Repeat until firm.) Now say that sentence with different words for **majority.** (Pause.) Get ready. (Signal.) *More than half of the class voted for Joyce.* (Repeat until firm.) (Repeat step 2 until firm.)

3. **Inquire.** (Pause.) What's a synonym for **inquire?** (Signal.) *Ask.* And what's a synonym for **ask?** (Signal.) *Inquire.* (Repeat step 3 until firm.)

4. Listen. "Where is the meeting?" he asked. Say that. (Signal.) *"Where is the meeting?" he asked.* (Repeat until firm.) Now say that sentence with a synonym for **asked.** (Pause.) Get ready. (Signal.) *"Where is the meeting?" he inquired.* (Repeat until firm.) (Repeat step 4 until firm.)

5. **Consume.** (Pause.) What does **consume** mean? (Signal.) *Use up.* What word means **use up?** (Signal.) *Consume.* (Repeat step 5 until firm.)

6. Listen. Every bath uses up thirty gallons of water. Say that. (Signal.) *Every bath uses up thirty gallons of water.* (Repeat until firm.) Now say that sentence using a different word for **uses up.** (Pause.) Get ready. (Signal.)

Every bath consumes thirty gallons of water. (Repeat until firm.) (Repeat step 6 until firm.)

======== EXERCISE 6 ========

BASIC EVIDENCE: Using Facts

The next Thinking Operation is Basic Evidence.

1. You're going to use two facts to explain things that happen. (Hold up one finger.) First fact. It takes many years to become a doctor. Say it. (Signal.) *It takes many years to become a doctor.* (Repeat until firm.) (Hold up two fingers.) Second fact. Doctors work in hospitals. Say it. (Signal.) *Doctors work in hospitals.* (Repeat until firm.)

2. Everybody, say those facts again. (Hold up one finger.) First fact. *It takes many years to become a doctor.* (Hold up two fingers.) Second fact. *Doctors work in hospitals.* (Repeat until the students say the facts in order.)

Individual test

Call on individual students to say the facts.

---

3. Here's what happens. They have to read hundreds of books. Tell me the fact that explains **why** that happens. (Pause.) Get ready. (Signal.) *It takes many years to become a doctor.*

4. Listen. First fact. It takes many years to become a doctor. Second fact. Doctors work in hospitals.

5. Here's what happens. There are no eighteen-year-old doctors. Tell me the fact that explains **why** that happens. (Pause.) Get ready. (Signal.) *It takes many years to become a doctor.*

6. Here's what happens. There are many nurses where doctors work. Tell me the fact that explains **why** that happens. (Pause.) Get ready. (Signal.) *Doctors work in hospitals.*

7. Here's what happens. Doctors hear ambulances every day. Tell me the fact that explains **why** that happens. (Pause.) Get ready. (Signal.) *Doctors work in hospitals.*

8. (Repeat steps 5–7 until firm.)

EXERCISE 7

SAME: Review

The next Thinking Operation is **Same.**

1. I'll name some things. When I call on you, name ways those things are the same.

2. A cow and a horse. (Call on one student.) Name eight ways they are the same. (Praise the student if he or she names eight ways.)

3. A television and a radio. (Call on one student.) Name eight ways they are the same. (Praise the student if he or she names eight ways.)

4. Skating and dancing. (Call on one student.) Name four ways they are the same. (Praise the student if he or she names four ways.)

5. A snake and a lizard. (Call on one student.) Name eight ways they are the same. (Praise the student if he or she names eight ways.)

EXERCISE 8

• **OPPOSITES**

The next Thinking Operation is **Opposites.**

1. (Draw a straight line on the board. Draw a jagged line below it. Point to the straight line.) This is straight.
   (Point to the crooked line.) This is crooked.

2. What's the opposite of **crooked?** (Signal.) *Straight.* What's the opposite of **straight?** (Signal.) *Crooked.*
   (Repeat step 2 until firm.)

EXERCISE 9

OPPOSITES

1. **Straight.** (Pause.) What's the opposite of **straight?** (Signal.) *Crooked.*
   Crooked. (Pause.) What's the opposite of **crooked?** (Signal.) *Straight.*
   (Repeat step 1 until firm.)

2. **Fuller.** (Pause.) What's the opposite of **fuller?** (Signal.) *Emptier.*
   Having a **noisy** party. (Pause.) What's the opposite of having a **noisy** party? (Signal.) *Having a quiet party.*
   (Repeat step 2 until firm.)

3. **Dead.** (Pause.) What's the opposite of **dead?** (Signal.) *Alive.*
   Hardest. (Pause.) What's the opposite of **hardest?** (Signal.) *Softest.*
   (Repeat step 3 until firm.)

4. **Straight.** (Pause.) What's the opposite of **straight?** (Signal.) *Crooked.*

5. (Repeat steps 2–4 until firm.)

> **Individual test**
> Call on individual students to do part of step 1, 2, or 3.

EXERCISE 10

OPPOSITES

1. You're going to say sentences with **opposites.**

2. Listen. Summer is usually the driest season. Say that. (Signal.) *Summer is usually the driest season.* (Repeat until firm.)
   Now say that sentence with the opposite of **driest.** (Pause.) Get ready. (Signal.) *Summer is usually the wettest season.* (Repeat until firm.)
   (Repeat step 2 until firm.)

3. Listen. Oak bark is rougher than beech bark. Say that. (Signal.) *Oak bark is rougher than beech bark.* (Repeat until firm.)
   Now say that sentence with the opposite of **rougher.** (Pause.) Get ready. (Signal.) *Oak bark is smoother than beech bark.* (Repeat until firm.)
   (Repeat step 3 until firm.)

4. Listen. Stoplights make driving safe. Say that. (Signal.) *Stoplights make driving safe.* (Repeat until firm.)
   Now say that sentence with the opposite of **safe.** (Pause.) Get ready. (Signal.) *Stoplights make driving dangerous.* (Repeat until firm.)
   (Repeat step 4 until firm.)

5. Listen. Some people are sad when they lose money. Say that. (Signal.) *Some people are sad when they lose money.* (Repeat until firm.)
Now say that sentence with the opposite of **sad.** (Pause.) Get ready. (Signal.) *Some people are happy when they lose money.* (Repeat until firm.)
(Repeat step 5 until firm.)

6. Listen. Good fruit is hard to find in winter. Say that. (Signal.) *Good fruit is hard to find in winter.* (Repeat until firm.)
Now say that sentence with the opposite of **good.** (Pause.) Get ready. (Signal.) *Bad fruit is hard to find in winter.* (Repeat until firm.)
(Repeat step 6 until firm.)

7. Listen. Most rivers are crooked. Say that. (Signal.) *Most rivers are crooked.* (Repeat until firm.)
Now say that sentence with the opposite of crooked. (Pause.) Get ready. (Signal.) *Most rivers are straight.* (Repeat until firm.)
(Repeat step 7 until firm.)

==================== EXERCISE 11 ====================

ANALOGIES: Synonyms

The next Thinking Operation is **Analogies.**

1. Here's an analogy about words. **Lazy** is to **indolent** as **complete** is to . . . (Pause 2 seconds.) Get ready. (Signal.) *Finish.*
Everybody, say that analogy. (Signal.) *Lazy is to indolent as complete is to finish.* (Repeat until firm.)

2. What are **lazy** and **complete?** (Signal.) *Words.*
To correct students who say *Synonyms:*
a. **Lazy** and **complete** are **words.**
b. (Repeat step 2.)
Lazy is to **indolent** as **complete** is to **finish.** That analogy tells something about those words. (Pause.) What does that analogy tell about those words? (Signal.) *What synonyms those words have.* (Repeat until firm.)

3. Say the analogy. (Signal.) *Lazy is to indolent as complete is to finish.* (Repeat until firm.)

4. And what does that analogy tell about those words? (Signal.) *What synonyms those words have.*

5. (Repeat steps 3 and 4 until firm.)

==================== EXERCISE 12 ====================

ANALOGIES: Opposites

1. Here's an analogy about words. **Short** is to **long** as **fast** is to . . . (Pause 2 seconds.) Get ready. (Signal.) *Slow.*
Everybody, say the analogy. (Signal.) *Short is to long as fast is to slow.* (Repeat until firm.)

2. What are **short** and **fast?** (Signal.) *Words.* **Short** is to **long** as **fast** is to **slow.** That analogy tells something about those words. (Pause.) What does that analogy tell about those words? (Signal.) *What opposites those words have.* (Repeat until firm.)

3. Say the analogy. (Signal.) *Short is to long as fast is to slow.* (Repeat until firm.)

4. And what does that analogy tell about those words? (Signal.) *What opposites those words have.*

5. (Repeat steps 3 and 4 until firm.)

==================== EXERCISE 13 ====================

ANALOGIES

> **Note:** Praise all reasonable responses in steps 1, 3, and 4, but have the group repeat the responses specified in the exercise.

Task A

1. Here's an analogy. A spoon is to metal as a toothbrush is to . . . (Pause 2 seconds.) Get ready. (Signal.) *Plastic.*

2. Everybody, say that analogy. (Signal.) *A spoon is to metal as a toothbrush is to plastic.* (Repeat until firm.)

3. What class are a spoon and a toothbrush in? (Signal.) *Tools.*

4. A spoon is to metal as a toothbrush is to plastic. The analogy tells something about those tools. (Pause.) What does that analogy tell about those tools? (Signal.) *What material those tools are made of.*
(Repeat step 4 until firm.)

5. Say the analogy. (Signal.) *A spoon is to metal as a toothbrush is to plastic.* (Repeat until firm.)

Task B

1. Here's an analogy. A ladder is to climbing as a shovel is to . . . (Pause 2 seconds.) Get ready. (Signal.) *Digging.*

2. Everybody, say that analogy. (Signal.) *A ladder is to climbing as a shovel is to digging.* (Repeat until firm.)

3. What class are a ladder and a shovel in? (Signal.) *Tools.*

4. A ladder is to climbing as a shovel is to digging. The analogy tells something about those tools. (Pause.) What does that analogy tell about those tools? (Signal.) *What you do with those tools.*
   (Repeat step 4 until firm.)

5. Say the analogy. (Signal.) *A ladder is to climbing as a shovel is to digging.* (Repeat until firm.)

EXERCISE 14

INDUCTIONS

The next Thinking Operation is **Inductions.**

1. I'm going to tell you facts about the sun and the temperature on planets. See if you can figure out the rules.

2. Listen. On Mercury the sun is near and the planet is hot. On Pluto the sun is far and the planet is cold. On Venus the sun is near and the planet is hot. On Neptune the sun is far and the planet is cold. On Jupiter the sun is far and the planet is cold.

3. Tell me the rule about what happens when the sun is far. (Pause.) Get ready. (Signal.) *When the sun is far, the planet is cold.*

4. Tell me the rule about what happens when the sun is near. (Pause.) Get ready. (Signal.) *When the sun is near, the planet is hot.*

5. (Repeat steps 3 and 4 until firm.)

> **Individual test**
> Call on individual students to do step 3 or 4.

Points

(Pass out the Workbooks.
Award points for Thinking Operations.)

WORKBOOK EXERCISES

We're going to do Workbooks now.

EXERCISE 15

DEDUCTIONS

1. Everybody, touch part A in your Workbook. ✔ Read the sentences in the box with me. Get ready. (Signal.) *Here's the only thing Sue did. Sue wore some of the white shirts.* What's the **only** thing Sue did? (Signal.) *Wore some of the white shirts.* (Repeat until firm.)

2. Everybody, read item 1 with me. Get ready. (Signal.) *Sue wore object 1.* Write the answer. (Wait.)

3. Read item 2 with me. Get ready. (Signal.) *Sue did not wear object 3.* Write the answer. (Wait.)

4. Read item 3 with me. Get ready. (Signal.) *Sue wore object 4.* Read the answer. (Wait.)

5. Get ready to check your answers. I'll read the items. You say **true, false,** or **maybe.**
   Item 1. Sue wore object 1. (Signal.) *Maybe.*
   Item 2. Sue did not wear object 3. (Signal.) *True.*
   Item 3. Sue wore object 4. (Signal.) *False.*

EXERCISE 16

SAME

1. Everybody, find part B in your Workbook. ✔ You're going to circle the answer at the end of each row.

2. Now, I'll read the words in each row. You circle the answer.

3. Row 1. **Motorcycle, ink, lamp.** Circle the answer. (Wait.)

4. Row 2. **Hot, sticky, lumpy.** Circle the answer. (Wait.)

5. Row 3. **Skates, water, picture.** Circle the answer. (Wait.)

6. Row 4. **Mean, happy, quick.** Circle the answer. (Wait.)

7. Row 5. **Envelope, flower, shell.** Circle the answer. (Wait.)

8. Get ready to check your answers. I'll read the words in each row. You tell me if the words name objects or actions, or tell what kind.
9. Row 1. **Motorcycle, ink, lamp.** (Signal.) *Objects.*
10. (Repeat step 9 for rows 2–5.)

═══ EXERCISE 17 ═══

ANALOGIES

1. Everybody, touch part C in your Workbook. ✔ I'll ready the analogy. Don't say the answer. Christmas is to **December** as Independence Day is to **blank.**
2. The words you'll choose from are **June, January,** and **July.** Listen to the analogy again and get ready to copy the right word in the blank. Christmas is to December as Independence Day is to **blank.** Copy the right word in the blank. (Wait.)
3. Listen. Christmas is to December as Independence Day is to blank. Everybody, what's the answer? (Signal.) *July.*
4. Everybody, say the whole analogy with me. (Signal.) *Christmas is to December as Independence Day is to July.* Put an X next to the analogy if you didn't copy the word **July.**
5. Listen. Christmas is to December as Independence Day is to July. That analogy tells something about those holidays. (Pause 4 seconds.)
   What does that analogy tell about those holidays? (Signal.) *What months those holidays are in.*

═══ EXERCISE 18 ═══

DESCRIPTION

1. Everybody, touch part D in your Workbook. ✔ Figure out which object I describe.
2. Item 1. This object is a living thing. This living thing is an animal. This animal is carnivorous. Listen again. (Repeat the description.) Write the letter for item 1.

3. Item 2. This object needs food. The object is found where it is hot. This is a herbivorous animal. Listen again. (Repeat the description.) Write the letter for item 2.
4. Item 3. This object is a living thing. This object is an animal. This animal lives where it is cold. Listen again. (Repeat the description.) Write the letter for item 3.
5. Let's check your answers. Mark any items you missed with an X.
6. Item 1. This object is a living thing. This living thing is an animal. This animal is carnivorous. Everybody, what letter? (Signal.) *B.* And what does **B** stand for? (Signal.) *A polar bear.*
7. (Repeat step 6 for items 2 and 3.)

Points
(Award points for Workbooks.)

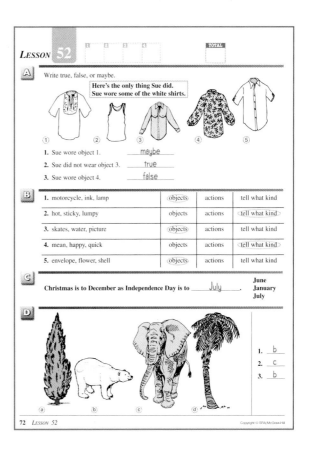

INFORMATION

We're going to work on Information now.

EXERCISE 19

MEMORIZATION: Poem
Say that poem we learned about the mechanic and the astronomer. Get ready. (Signal.)

A mechanic fixes cars;
An astronomer looks at stars;
A captain has two bars;
And a boxer spars and spars.
(Repeat until firm.)

> *Individual test*
> Call on individual students to say the whole poem.

EXERCISE 20

MEMORIZATION: Poem
Say that poem we learned about the beautician and the tailor. Get ready. (Signal.)

A beautician fixes hair;
A tailor can mend a tear;
An exposition is a fair;
And one plus one is a pair.

> *Individual test*
> Call on individual students to say the whole poem.

Points
(Award points for Information.
Have the students add up their daily total.)

END OF LESSON 52

1	2	3	4

TOTAL

 A   Write true, false, or maybe.

> **Here's the only thing Sue did.**
> **Sue wore some of the white shirts.**

① ② ③ ④ ⑤

1. Sue wore object 1. _____

2. Sue did not wear object 3. _____

3. Sue wore object 4. _____

 B

1. motorcycle, ink, lamp	objects	actions	tell what kind
2. hot, sticky, lumpy	objects	actions	tell what kind
3. skates, water, picture	objects	actions	tell what kind
4. mean, happy, quick	objects	actions	tell what kind
5. envelope, flower, shell	objects	actions	tell what kind

 C

Christmas is to December as Independence Day is to _____.

June
January
July

D

ⓐ ⓑ ⓒ ⓓ

1. _____
2. _____
3. _____

Lesson 52 from Comprehension A Workbook

► Comprehension B1— Lesson 13

Some of the activities in the early part of **Comprehension B1** are similar to activities in **Comprehension A.** For example, analogies (Exercise 2), classification (Exercise 3), and statement inference (Exercise 4) consolidate information presented in **Comprehension A.** Also, the workbook deductions exercise (Exercise 6) is a variation of a **Comprehension A** activity.

The new material taught in **Comprehension B1** includes the following.

▲ New definitions (Exercises 1 and 5)

▲ Parts of speech. By Lesson 13, verbs and nouns have already been taught. Adjectives are introduced in Exercise 7.

▲ New following-directions tasks (Exercise 8)

▲ Definitions in which students complete sentences with forms of a vocabulary word

The main difference between **Comprehension A** and **Comprehension B1** is the number of independent activities the students perform. In Lesson 13, students independently do exercises that require them to identify verbs and nouns, use basic evidence to explain why different events happened, answer questions that are based on a statement, and identify parts of a skeleton (using information that has been taught starting in Lesson 3).

Correction Reminder
Follow these steps to correct errors.

1. (Say the answer.)

2. (Repeat the task [the instruction or wording of the question].)

3. (Back up in the exercise and present the steps in order.)

4. (Finish the remaining steps in the exercise.)

5. (Repeat the entire exercise if students made more than one or two mistakes.)

ORAL GROUP WORK

━━━━━━ EXERCISE 1 ━━━━━━

DEFINITIONS

1. Complete each sentence by saying **select, selected,** or **selecting.**

2. Listen. The man will **blank** a shirt. What word? (Signal.) *Select.* Say the sentence. (Signal.) *The man will select a shirt.*

3. Listen. The man has **blank** a shirt. What word? (Signal.) *Selected.* Say the sentence. (Signal.) *The man has selected a shirt.*

4. Listen. The man has to **blank** a shirt. What word? (Signal.) *Select.* Say the sentence. (Signal.) *The man has to select a shirt.*

5. Listen. You must **blank** a shirt. What word? (Signal.) *Select.* Say the sentence. (Signal.) *You must select a shirt.*

6. Listen. They are **blank** a shirt. What word? (Signal.) *Selecting.* Say the sentence. (Signal.) *They are selecting a shirt.*

7. Listen. They are not **blank** a shirt. What word? (Signal.) *Selecting.* Say the sentence. (Signal.) *They are not selecting a shirt.*

8. (Repeat steps 1–7 until firm.)

━━━━━━ EXERCISE 2 ━━━━━━

● **ANALOGIES**

1. **Analogies** tell how things are the same. Listen to this analogy: A **bird** is to **flying** as a **fish** is to **swimming.**

2. Listen to the first part. A **bird** is to **flying.** Say that. (Signal.) (Repeat until firm.)

3. Listen to both parts. A **bird** is to **flying** as a **fish** is to **swimming.** Say the whole analogy with me. (Signal. Respond with the students.) (Repeat until firm.)

4. All by yourselves. Say the whole analogy. (Signal.) (Repeat until firm.)

5. That analogy tells one way that a bird and a fish are the same. Everybody, what class are a bird and a fish in? (Signal.) *Animals.* Yes, animals.

6. The analogy tells something about each animal. Listen. A **bird** is to **flying** as a **fish** is to **swimming.** Flying is how a bird **moves.** Swimming is how a fish **moves.** So, the analogy tells how each animal **moves.**

7. What does the analogy tell? (Signal.) *How each animal moves.*
   (Repeat step 7 until firm.)

8. Get ready to tell how some other animals **move.** A **bird** is to **flying,** as a **fish** is to **swimming,** as a **frog** is to . . . (Pause.) Get ready. (Signal.) *Hopping.* As a **horse** is to . . . (Pause.) Get ready. (Signal.) *Running.*
   (Repeat step 8 until firm.)

┌───┐
│ *Individual test*   │
│ Repeat step 8 with individual students. │
└───┘

━━━━━━ EXERCISE 3 ━━━━━━

CLASSIFICATION

1. Name some things that are in the class of clothing. (Call on a student.) Name some things that are in the class of buildings. (Call on a student.) Name some things that are in the class of living things. (Call on a student.)

2. Tell me if the thing I name is in the class of **clothing, buildings,** or **living things.**
   Garage. (Pause.) What class? (Signal.) *Buildings.*
   Flower. (Pause.) What class? (Signal.) *Living things.*
   Shed. (Pause.) What class? (Signal.) *Buildings.*
   Socks. (Pause.) What class? (Signal.) *Clothing.*
   Shoe. (Pause.) What class? (Signal.) *Clothing.*
   Apartment. (Pause.) What class? (Signal.) *Buildings.*
   Alligator. (Pause.) What class? (Signal.) *Living things.*
   Cap. (Pause.) What class? (Signal.) *Clothing.*
   Tree. (Pause.) What class? (Signal.) *Living things.*

EXERCISE 4

STATEMENT INFERENCE

1. Get ready to answer questions about a sentence. Listen. Nearly all words have a consonant. Say that. (Signal.) (Repeat until firm.)

2. How many words have a consonant? (Signal.) *Nearly all.*
   Do all words have a vowel? (Signal.) *Maybe.*
   Do only a few words have a consonant? (Signal.) *No.*
   Do all words have a consonant? (Signal.) *No.*
   What do nearly all words have? (Signal.) *A consonant.*
   What things have a consonant? (Signal.) *Nearly all words.*
   (Repeat step 2 until firm.)

> **Individual test**
> Repeat step 2 with individual students.

EXERCISE 5

● DEFINITIONS

1. What word means **guard?** (Signal.) *Protect.*
   What part of speech is **protect?** (Signal.) *A verb.* What's the noun that comes from **protect?** (Signal.) *Protection.*
   (Repeat step 1 until firm.)

2. I'll say some sentences. Then I'll ask you the part of speech for one of the words. Listen. He wanted more **protection** from the angry mob. What part of speech is **protection?** (Signal.) *Noun.*
   Listen. The rubber suit **protected** her from the cold water. What part of speech is **protected?** (Signal.) *Verb.*
   Listen. Helmets **protect** the players' heads. What part of speech is **protect?** (Signal.) *Verb.*
   Listen. The goggles were good **protection** for his eyes. What part of speech is **protection?** (Signal.) *Noun.*
   (Repeat step 2 until firm.)

> **Individual test**
> Repeat step 2 with individual students.

WORKBOOK EXERCISES

> **Note:** Pass out the Workbooks.

EXERCISE 6

● DEDUCTIONS

1. Open your Workbook to Lesson 13. ✔ I'll read the instructions for part A. Complete the **deductions.**

2. (Call on a student to read item 1.) *Every person has a skull. John is a person.* Everybody, complete that deduction. (Signal.) *So, John has a skull.*

3. (Call on a student to read item 2.) *Some animals have bones. Snakes are animals.* Everybody, complete that deduction. (Signal.) *So, maybe snakes have bones.*

4. You'll do the items later.

EXERCISE 7

● PARTS OF SPEECH

Task A

1. What part of speech names persons, places, or things? (Signal.) *Nouns.* What part of speech tells the action that things do? (Signal.) *Verbs.* What part of speech are the words **is, was,** and **have?** (Signal.) *Verbs.*

2. The next part of speech is **adjectives.** Here's a rule about adjectives. Any words that come before a noun and tell about the noun are called adjectives. Words that tell **how many** or **what kind** are adjectives. What are words that come before a noun and tell about the noun? (Signal.) *Adjectives.*

3. The word **cat** is a noun. Listen. **The cat.** The word **the** is an adjective because it comes before the noun and tells about the noun.

4. Listen. **That cat.** What's the adjective? (Signal.) *That.*

5. Listen. **That fat cat.** There are two adjectives. What's the first adjective? (Signal.) *That.* What's the second adjective? (Signal.) *Fat.*

6. Listen. **Five cats.** What's the adjective? (Signal.) *Five.*

7. Listen. **Five mean cats.** What's the first adjective? (Signal.) *Five.* What's the second adjective? (Signal.) *Mean.*

Task B

1. Look at part B. The nouns are underlined in each sentence.

2. Sentence 1. **Six cats played.** What's the **noun?** (Signal.) *Cats.*
   What's the **adjective?** (Signal.) *Six.*

3. Sentence 2. **That dog jumped.** What's the **noun?** (Signal.) *Dog.*
   What's the **adjective?** (Signal.) *That.*

4. Sentence 3. **That big dog jumped.** What's the **noun?** (Signal.) *Dog.*
   What's the **first adjective?** (Signal.) *That.*
   What's the **next adjective?** (Signal.) *Big.*

5. Sentence 4. **A big dog jumped.** What's the **noun?** (Signal.) *Dog.*
   What's the **first adjective?** (Signal.) *A.*
   What's the **next adjective?** (Signal.) *Big.*

6. Sentence 5. **An old black cat ran.** What's the **noun?** (Signal.) *Cat.*
   What's the **first adjective?** (Signal.) *An.*
   What's the **next adjective?** (Signal.) *Old.*
   What's the **next adjective?** (Signal.) *Black.*

7. Sentence 6. **Ten sheep slept.** What's the **noun?** (Signal.) *Sheep.*
   What's the **adjective?** (Signal.) *Ten.*

8. Sentence 7. **Six men sat.** What's the **noun?** (Signal.) *Men.*
   What's the **adjective?** (Signal.) *Six.*

9. Sentence 8. **A red truck crashed.** What's the **noun?** (Signal.) *Truck.*
   What's the **first adjective?** (Signal.) *A.*
   What's the **next adjective?** (Signal.) *Red.*

10. (Repeat steps 2–9 until firm.)

11. I'll read the instructions for part B. Draw a line **over** the adjectives. Do the items now. (Wait.)

Task C

1. Let's check your work. Put an **X** next to any item you miss.

2. (Call on a student.) Read sentence 1. *Six cats played.* What did you make a line over? *Six.*

3. (Repeat step 2 for sentences 2–8.)

Answer key **2.** *That* **3.** *That, big* **4.** *A, big* **5.** *An, old, black* **6.** *Ten* **7.** *Six* **8.** *A, red*

=== EXERCISE 8 ===

FOLLOWING DIRECTIONS

1. Look at part C. I'll read the instructions. Fill in each blank. Then do what the sentence tells you to do.

2. Everybody, touch the first blank. ✔ What is under that blank? (Signal.) *Glaf.* Find **glaf** in the list. (Wait.) What does **glaf** mean? (Signal.) *Write.* So, write the word **write** in the blank above **glaf.** (Wait.)

3. You'll fill in the rest of the blanks later. Be sure to do what the sentence tells you to do.

=== EXERCISE 9 ===

DEFINITIONS

1. (Call on a student to read the instructions for part D.) *Write a word that comes from obtain in each blank.*

2. (Call on a student to read item 1.) *The robber will blank a robe for his back.* Everybody, what word goes in the blank? (Signal.) *Obtain.*

3. (Call on a student to read item 2.) *The ram wants to blank some tin cans to eat.* Everybody, what word goes in the blank? (Signal.) *Obtain.*

4. (Call on a student to read item 3.) *The man has blank a pig for a pet.* Everybody, what word goes in the blank? (Signal.) *Obtained.*

5. (Call on a student to read item 4.) *Six shoppers are blank ten socks.* Everybody, what word goes in the blank? (Signal.) *Obtaining.*

6. (Call on a student to read item 5.) *Ten socks were blank by six shoppers.* Everybody, what word goes in the blank? (Signal.) *Obtained.*

7. You'll do the items later.

LESSON 13

Points
(Award points for Oral Work.)

Completing the Workbook Lesson
Do the rest of the Workbook lesson now. If you finish early, write a story about today's picture. (Wait.)

Workcheck
1. Exchange Workbooks and get ready to check the answers. (Wait.) Put an **X** next to any item the person misses. (Call on individual students to read each item and its answer.)
2. Figure out the person's Workbook points, and then return the Workbook. (Wait.)

Points
(Award bonus points.
Have students total their points and enter the total on the Point Summary Chart.)

END OF LESSON 13

LESSON 13

E Circle the verbs.
Underline the nouns.

1. His mom constructed a shed.
2. His mom has constructed that shed.
3. Six men will obtain ten socks.
4. The shoppers will be shopping for hats.
5. A cop was mopping with a mop.
6. Three men are mopping rocks with that mop.
7. A metal ship is rocking in the deep pond.
8. That shop has sold hats and socks.

F Write the number of the fact that explains why each thing happened.

  1. A robber stole Ted's wallet.
  2. Cops got the robber.

a. They sent him to prison.   2
b. He ran to the cops.   1
c. He had no cash in his pocket.   1
d. He had to give the wallet back.   2

G Read the sentence and answer the questions.

If it is an insect, it does not have bones.

1. What happens if it is an insect?
   It does not have bones.
2. What do insects not have?
   Bones
3. Do insects have ribs?
   No
4. Does a bee have bones?
   No
5. What does not have bones?
   An insect

30 *Lesson 13*   Copyright © SRA/McGraw-Hill

ERRORS   **LESSON 13**

A Complete the deductions.

1. Every person has a skull.
   John is a person.
   So, John has a skull.

2. Some animals have bones.
   Snakes are animals.
   So, maybe snakes have bones.

3. Insects do not have spines.
   Antelopes are mammals.
   So, nothing.

4. John has every kind of bone.
   Ribs are bones.
   So, John has ribs.

B Draw a line over the adjectives.

1. Six cats played.
2. That dog jumped.
3. That big dog jumped.
4. A big dog jumped.
5. An old black cat ran.
6. Ten sheep slept.
7. Six men sat.
8. A red truck crashed.

C Fill in each blank. Then do what the sentence tells you to do.

Write	the	word
glaf	ag	preb
man	on	the
rop	k	wid
line		
hux		

ag—the
hux—line
preb—word
rop—man   man
wid—the
glaf—write
k—on

D Write a word that comes from **obtain** in each blank.

1. The robber will _obtain_ a robe for his back.
2. The ram wants to _obtain_ some tin cans to eat.
3. The man has _obtained_ a pig for a pet.
4. Six shoppers are _obtaining_ ten socks.
5. Ten socks were _obtained_ by six shoppers.

Copyright © SRA/McGraw-Hill   *Lesson 13* **29**

LESSON 13

H Fill in each blank.

1. humerus
2. femur
3. ribs
4. spine
5. skull
6. pelvis

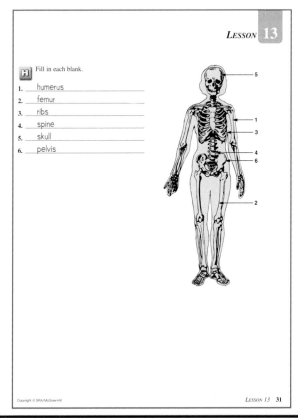

Copyright © SRA/McGraw-Hill   *Lesson 13* **31**

Lesson 13 from Comprehension B1 TPB

A Complete the deductions.

1. Every person has a skull.
   John is a person.

   _____

2. Some animals have bones.
   Snakes are animals.

   _____

3. Insects do not have spines.
   Antelopes are mammals.

   _____

4. John has every kind of bone.
   Ribs are bones.

   _____

B Draw a line over the adjectives.

1. Six <u>cats</u> played.
2. That <u>dog</u> jumped.
3. That big <u>dog</u> jumped.
4. A big <u>dog</u> jumped.
5. An old black <u>cat</u> ran.
6. Ten <u>sheep</u> slept.
7. Six <u>men</u> sat.
8. A red <u>truck</u> crashed.

C Fill in each blank. Then do what the sentence tells you to do.

_____	_____	_____
glaf	ag	preb

_____	_____	_____
rop	k	wid

_____
hux

ag—the
hux—line
preb—word
rop—man
wid—the
glaf—write
k—on

_____

D Write a word that comes from **obtain** in each blank.

1. The robber will _____
   a robe for his back.

2. The ram wants to _____
   some tin cans to eat.

3. The man has _____
   a pig for a pet.

4. Six shoppers are _____
   ten socks.

5. Ten socks were _____
   by six shoppers.

E Circle the verbs.
Underline the nouns.

1. His mom constructed a shed.

2. His mom has constructed that shed.

3. Six men will obtain ten socks.

4. The shoppers will be shopping for hats.

5. A cop was mopping with a mop.

6. Three men are mopping rocks with that mop.

7. A metal ship is rocking in the deep pond.

8. That shop has sold hats and socks.

F Write the number of the fact that explains why each thing happened.

1. **A robber stole Ted's wallet.**

2. **Cops got the robber.**

a. They sent him to prison. _____

b. He ran to the cops. _____

c. He had no cash in his pocket. _____

d. He had to give the wallet back. _____

G Read the sentence and answer the questions.

If it is an insect, it does not have bones.

1. What happens if it is an insect?

_____

2. What do insects not have?

_____

3. Do insects have ribs?

_____

4. Does a bee have bones?

_____

5. What does not have bones?

_____

Lesson 13 from Comprehension B1 Workbook

H Fill in each blank.

1. _____

2. _____

3. _____

4. _____

5. _____

6. _____

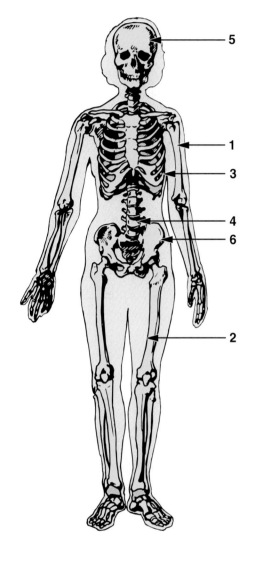

Lesson 13 from Comprehension B1 Workbook

Comprehension B2— Lesson 52

Many of the same tracks that appeared in Lesson 13 of **Comprehension B1** still appear in **Comprehension B2,** Lesson 52; however, new and more complex examples are used in Lesson 52.

▲ The definitions activities deal with three forms of a word—noun, verb, and adjective

▲ The once-simple rules have been replaced by basic economics rules, such as "Products that are readier to use cost more."

▲ Students have learned eight different ways to combine sentences; the latest way uses the word **however** (Exercise 3)

▲ Editing activities focus on basic punctuation errors and identifying redundant sentences

The independent activities include the following.

■ Using rules as the basis for drawing inferences about the human body, including which tubes are arteries, which tubes are veins, and which gas the blood in each tube carries

■ Using different inflections for verbs

■ Answering questions about a story. This is a variation of an activity that involved a single sentence in Lesson 13. The story presents a new rule. Both literal and indirect questions are used. Note that students indicate whether each question is answered by words in the story or whether a deduction is required.

■ Writing similes based on the sameness of objects

■ Rewriting a paragraph, applying the sentence-combination skills that have been taught

■ Following precise directions to construct a drawing

■ Rewriting combined sentences contained in a passage as separate sentences

■ Reviewing the parts of speech that have been taught—noun, verb, adjective

ORAL GROUP WORK

———— **EXERCISE 1** ————

DEFINITIONS

Task A

1. Tell me the word that means **get.** (Pause.)
   Get ready. (Signal.) *Acquire.*
   What part of speech is **acquire?**
   (Signal.) *A verb.*

   (Write on the board:) **acquisition**

2. (Point to **acquisition**.) Here's a noun that comes from the verb **acquire. Acquisition.**
   What word? (Signal.) *Acquisition.*
   An acquisition is **something you acquire.**

3. I'll say some sentences that have a **blank** in them. Complete each sentence by saying **acquisition** or **acquisitions.** Listen. The boat was an expensive **blank.** (Pause.)
   What word? (Signal.) *Acquisition.* Say the sentence. (Signal.) *The boat was an expensive acquisition.*

4. Listen. He made several **blank** at the store. (Pause.) What word? (Signal.) *Acquisitions.* Say the sentence. (Signal.) *He made several acquisitions at the store.*

5. Listen. A TV set is a popular **blank.** (Pause.) What word? (Signal.) *Acquisition.* Say the sentence. (Signal.) *A TV set is a popular acquisition.*

6. Listen. She protected her one new **blank.** (Pause.) What word? (Signal.) *Acquisition.* Say the sentence. (Signal.) *She protected her one new acquisition.*

7. (Repeat steps 3–6 until firm.)

Task B

1. What part of speech is **acquisition?**
   (Signal.) *A noun.*
   What part of speech is **acquire?**
   (Signal.) *A verb.*

2. Verbs have different endings. **Acquired** is a verb. **Are acquiring** is a verb. **Acquires** is a verb. Is **acquisition** a verb? (Signal.) *No.*
   What part of speech is **acquisition?** (Signal.) *A noun.*

3. I'll say some words. You tell me if what I say is a noun or a verb.
   Is acquiring. Say it. (Signal.)
   What part of speech? (Signal.) *Verb.*
   Acquired. Say it. (Signal.)
   What part of speech? (Signal.) *Verb.*
   Acquires. Say it. (Signal.)
   What part of speech? (Signal.) *Verb.*
   Acquisition. Say it. (Signal.)
   What part of speech? (Signal.) *Noun.*
   Were acquiring. Say it. (Signal.)
   What part of speech? (Signal.) *Verb.*
   (Repeat step 3 until firm.)

> *Individual test*
> Repeat step 3 with individual students.

WORKBOOK EXERCISES

Note: Pass out the Workbooks.

═══ **EXERCISE 2** ═══

INFORMATION: Economics Rules

(Write on the board:)
Products that are readier to use cost more.

1. Here's a new rule. Products that are readier to use cost more. Say that rule. (Signal.) (Repeat until firm.)
2. A ready-made skirt is readier to use than material and a pattern. Here's why. The ready-made skirt is ready to wear, but material and a pattern aren't.
3. Tell me which is readier to use, a ready-made skirt or material and a pattern. (Pause.) Get ready. (Signal.) *A ready-made skirt.* Why? (Call on a student. Accept a reasonable response, such as: *A ready-made skirt is ready to wear, but material and a pattern aren't.*)
Tell me which is readier to use, a model you have to put together or a model that is already put together. (Pause.) Get ready. (Signal.) *A model that is already put together.* **Why?** (Call on a student. Accept a reasonable response, such as: *A model that is already put together is ready to play with, but the model you have to put together isn't.*)
Tell me which is readier to use, frozen French fries or cooked French fries. (Pause.) Get ready. (Signal.) *Cooked French fries.* Why? (Call on a student. Accept a reasonable response, such as: *Cooked French fries are ready to eat; frozen French fries aren't.*)
(Repeat step 3 until firm.)
4. Open your Workbook to Lesson 52. ✔ Look at part A. Get ready to answer the questions.
5. What's the rule about products that are readier to use? (Signal.) *Products that are readier to use cost more.* (Repeat until firm.)

6. Which is readier to use, a ready-made skirt or material and a pattern? (Signal.) *A ready-made skirt.*
So, what else do you know about a ready-made skirt? (Signal.) *It costs more.*
How do you know? (Signal.) *Because it's readier to use.*
(Repeat step 6 until firm.)
7. Which costs more, a model that you have to put together or a model that is already put together? (Signal.) *A model that is already put together.* How do you know? (Signal.) *Because it's readier to use.*
(Repeat step 7 until firm.)
8. Mrs. Anderson obtains 5 pounds of frozen French fries. Mrs. Miller obtains 5 pounds of cooked French fries. Whose French fries cost more? (Signal.) *Mrs. Miller's.* How do you know? (Signal.) *Because they're readier to use.*
(Repeat step 8 until firm.)
9. You'll write the items later.

═══ **EXERCISE 3** ═══

SENTENCE COMBINATIONS

1. (Call on a student to read the instructions for part B.) *Combine the sentences with however.*
2. (Call on a student to read item 1.) *The man modified his car. His car still did not run.*
Everybody, say the combined sentence with **however.** (Pause.) Get ready. (Signal.) *The man modified his car; however, it still did not run.* (Repeat until firm.)
3. Let's go over the rules. What must every written sentence **begin with?** (Signal.) *A capital letter.*
What must every written sentence **have?** (Signal.) *An end mark.*
What mark do you put before **however?** (Signal.) *A semicolon.*
What mark do you put after **however?** (Signal.) *A comma.*
Name **four** words that you put commas **before.** (Call on a student.)
Who, which, but, particularly.
(Repeat step 3 until firm.)
4. You'll do the items later.

═══ EXERCISE 4 ═══

● **EDITING**

1. I'll read the instructions for part C. Underline the redundant sentences. Circle and correct the punctuation errors. A punctuation error occurs when a period, comma, or semicolon is missing or is used wrong.

2. I'll read the story. Say "Stop" as soon as I read a sentence that is redundant or that has a punctuation error. A bell rang. Sam put on his firefighter's hat and his firefighter's coat. *Stop.*

   What's wrong with that sentence? (Call on a student. Accept a reasonable response, such as: *It doesn't have a period.*)

   Everybody, make a circle at the end of the sentence and put a period inside the circle. (Wait.)

3. He jumped on the fire truck as it roared out of the station. Sam was a firefighter. *Stop.*

   What's wrong with that sentence? (Call on a student. Accept a reasonable response, such as: *It's redundant because we already know Sam is a firefighter.*) Everybody, underline that sentence. (Wait.)

4. The truck sped down Oak Street and screeched around, the corner of Oak and First. *Stop.*

   What's wrong with that sentence? (Call on a student. Accept a reasonable response, such as: *You don't need a comma between around and the.*) Everybody, circle the comma and then cross the comma out. (Wait.)

5. You'll finish part C later.

Points

(Award points for Oral Work.)

Completing the Workbook Lesson

Do the Workbook lesson now. If you finish early, write a story about today's picture. (Wait.)

Workcheck

1. Exchange Workbooks and get ready to check the answers. (Wait.)

   Put an **X** next to any item the person misses. (Call on individual students to read each item and its answer.)

2. Figure out the person's Workbook points, and then return the Workbook. (Wait.)

Points

(Award bonus points.

Have students total their points and enter the total on the Point Summary Chart.)

Note: Tell the students to bring lined paper to class tomorrow.

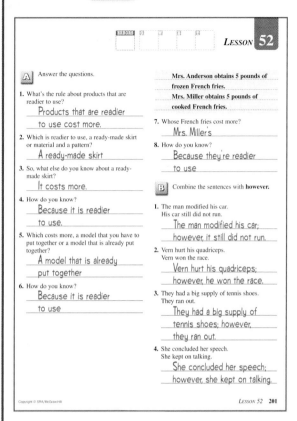

A Answer the questions.

1. What's the rule about products that are readier to use?
   Products that are readier to use cost more.

2. Which is readier to use, a ready-made skirt or material and a pattern?
   A ready-made skirt

3. So, what else do you know about a ready-made skirt?
   It costs more.

4. How do you know?
   Because it is readier to use.

5. Which costs more, a model that you have to put together or a model that is already put together?
   A model that is already put together

6. How do you know?
   Because it is readier to use.

Mrs. Anderson obtains 5 pounds of frozen French fries.
Mrs. Miller obtains 5 pounds of cooked French fries.

7. Whose French fries cost more?
   Mrs. Miller's

8. How do you know?
   Because they're readier to use

B Combine the sentences with **however**.

1. The man modified his car.
   His car still did not run.
   The man modified his car; however, it still did not run.

2. Vern hurt his quadriceps.
   Vern won the race.
   Vern hurt his quadriceps; however, he won the race.

3. They had a big supply of tennis shoes.
   They ran out.
   They had a big supply of tennis shoes; however, they ran out.

4. She concluded her speech.
   She kept on talking.
   She concluded her speech; however, she kept on talking.

Copyright © SRA/McGraw-Hill
LESSON 52 201

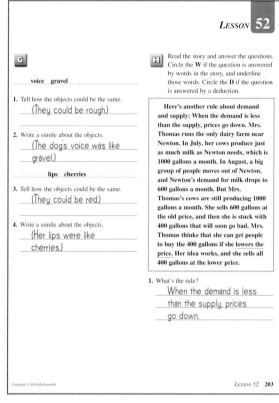

G

voice   gravel

1. Tell how the objects could be the same.
   (They could be rough.)

2. Write a simile about the objects.
   (The dog's voice was like gravel.)

lips   cherries

3. Tell how the objects could be the same.
   (They could be red.)

4. Write a simile about the objects.
   (Her lips were like cherries.)

H Read the story and answer the questions. Circle the **W** if the question is answered by words in the story, and underline those words. Circle the **D** if the question is answered by a deduction.

Here's another rule about demand and supply: When the demand is less than the supply, prices go down. Mrs. Thomas runs the only dairy farm near Newton. In July, her cows produce just as much milk as Newton needs, which is 1000 gallons a month. In August, a big group of people moves out of Newton, and Newton's demand for milk drops to 600 gallons a month. But Mrs. Thomas's cows are still producing 1000 gallons a month. She sells 600 gallons at the old price, and then she is stuck with 400 gallons that will soon go bad. Mrs. Thomas thinks that she can get people to buy the 400 gallons if she lowers the price. Her idea works, and she sells all 400 gallons at the lower price.

1. What's the rule?
   When the demand is less than the supply, prices go down.

Copyright © SRA/McGraw-Hill
LESSON 52 203

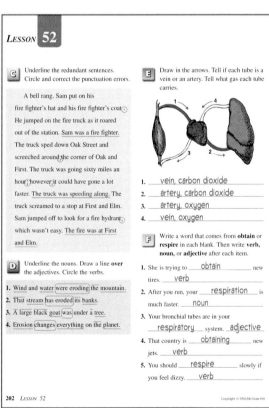

C Underline the redundant sentences. Circle and correct the punctuation errors.

A bell rang. Sam put on his fire fighter's hat and his fire fighter's coat. He jumped on the fire truck as it roared out of the station. Sam was a fire fighter. The truck sped down Oak Street and screeched around the corner of Oak and First. The truck was going sixty miles an hour; however, it could have gone a lot faster. The truck was speeding along. The truck screamed to a stop at First and Elm. Sam jumped off to look for a fire hydrant, which wasn't easy. The fire was at First and Elm.

D Underline the nouns. Draw a line **over** the adjectives. Circle the verbs.

1. Wind and water were eroding the mountain.
2. That stream has eroded its banks.
3. A large black goat was under a tree.
4. Erosion changes everything on the planet.

E Draw in the arrows. Tell if each tube is a vein or an artery. Tell what gas each tube carries.

1. vein, carbon dioxide
2. artery, carbon dioxide
3. artery, oxygen
4. vein, oxygen

F Write a word that comes from **obtain** or **respire** in each blank. Then write **verb**, **noun**, or **adjective** after each item.

1. She is trying to obtain new tires. verb
2. After you run, your respiration is much faster. noun
3. Your bronchial tubes are in your respiratory system. adjective
4. That country is obtaining new jets. verb
5. You should respire slowly if you feel dizzy. verb

202 LESSON 52
Copyright © SRA/McGraw-Hill

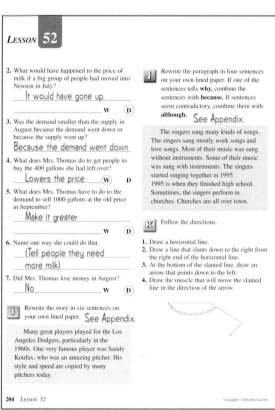

2. What would have happened to the price of milk if a big group of people had moved into Newton in July?
   It would have gone up.
                                    W   D

3. Was the demand smaller than the supply in August because the demand went down or because the supply went up?
   Because the demand went down

4. What does Mrs. Thomas do to get people to buy the 400 gallons she had left over?
   Lowers the price   W   D

5. What does Mrs. Thomas have to do to the demand to sell 1000 gallons at the old price in September?
   Make it greater
                                    W   D

6. Name one way she could do that.
   (Tell people they need more milk)

7. Did Mrs. Thomas lose money in August?
   No   W   D

I Rewrite the story in six sentences on your own lined paper. See Appendix.

Many great players played for the Los Angeles Dodgers, particularly in the 1960s. One very famous player was Sandy Koufax, who was an amazing pitcher. His style and speed are copied by many pitchers today.

J Rewrite the paragraph in four sentences on your own lined paper. If one of the sentences tells **why**, combine the sentences with **because**. If sentences seem contradictory, combine them with **although**. See Appendix.

The singers sang many kinds of songs. The singers sang mostly work songs and love songs. Most of their music was sung without instruments. Some of their music was sung with instruments. The singers started singing together in 1995. 1995 is when they finished high school. Sometimes, the singers perform in churches. Churches are all over town.

K Follow the directions.

1. Draw a horizontal line.
2. Draw a line that slants down to the right from the right end of the horizontal line.
3. At the bottom of the slanted line, draw an arrow that points down to the left.
4. Draw the muscle that will move the slanted line in the direction of the arrow.

204 LESSON 52
Copyright © SRA/McGraw-Hill

END OF LESSON 52

210 LESSON 52

Lesson 52 from Comprehension B2 TPB

A Answer the questions.

1. What's the rule about products that are readier to use?

_____

_____

2. Which is readier to use, a ready-made skirt or material and a pattern?

_____

3. So, what else do you know about a ready-made skirt?

_____

4. How do you know?

_____

_____

5. Which costs more, a model that you have to put together or a model that is already put together?

_____

_____

6. How do you know?

_____

_____

Mrs. Anderson obtains 5 pounds of frozen French fries.

Mrs. Miller obtains 5 pounds of cooked French fries.

7. Whose French fries cost more?

_____

8. How do you know?

_____

_____

B Combine the sentences with **however.**

1. The man modified his car.
   His car still did not run.

_____

_____

2. Vern hurt his quadriceps.
   Vern won the race.

_____

_____

3. They had a big supply of tennis shoes.
   They ran out.

_____

_____

4. She concluded her speech.
   She kept on talking.

_____

_____

C Underline the redundant sentences. Circle and correct the punctuation errors.

A bell rang. Sam put on his fire fighter's hat and his fire fighter's coat He jumped on the fire truck as it roared out of the station. Sam was a fire fighter. The truck sped down Oak Street and screeched around the corner of Oak and First. The truck was going sixty miles an hour however it could have gone a lot faster. The truck was speeding along. The truck screamed to a stop at First and Elm. Sam jumped off to look for a fire hydrant which wasn't easy. The fire was at First and Elm.

D Underline the nouns. Draw a line **over** the adjectives. Circle the verbs.

1. Wind and water were eroding the mountain.
2. That stream has eroded its banks.
3. A large black goat was under a tree.
4. Erosion changes everything on the planet.

E Draw in the arrows. Tell if each tube is a vein or an artery. Tell what gas each tube carries.

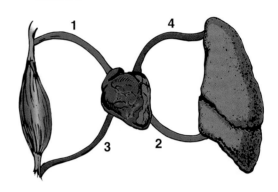

1. _____
2. _____
3. _____
4. _____

F Write a word that comes from **obtain** or **respire** in each blank. Then write **verb, noun,** or **adjective** after each item.

1. She is trying to _____ new tires. _____

2. After you run, your _____ is much faster. _____

3. Your bronchial tubes are in your _____ system. _____

4. That country is _____ new jets. _____

5. You should _____ slowly if you feel dizzy. _____

Lesson 52 from Comprehension B2 Workbook

G

---

voice   gravel

---

1. Tell how the objects could be the same.

_____

_____

2. Write a simile about the objects.

_____

_____

lips   cherries

---

3. Tell how the objects could be the same.

_____

_____

4. Write a simile about the objects.

_____

_____

H Read the story and answer the questions. Circle the **W** if the question is answered by words in the story, and underline those words. Circle the **D** if the question is answered by a deduction.

> Here's another rule about demand and supply: When the demand is less than the supply, prices go down. Mrs. Thomas runs the only dairy farm near Newton. In July, her cows produce just as much milk as Newton needs, which is 1000 gallons a month. In August, a big group of people moves out of Newton, and Newton's demand for milk drops to 600 gallons a month. But Mrs. Thomas's cows are still producing 1000 gallons a month. She sells 600 gallons at the old price, and then she is stuck with 400 gallons that will soon go bad. Mrs. Thomas thinks that she can get people to buy the 400 gallons if she lowers the price. Her idea works, and she sells all 400 gallons at the lower price.

1. What's the rule?

_____

_____

_____

2. What would have happened to the price of milk if a big group of people had moved into Newton in July?

_____

_____ **W**   **D**

3. Was the demand smaller than the supply in August because the demand went down or because the supply went up?

_____

_____

4. What does Mrs. Thomas do to get people to buy the 400 gallons she had left over?

_____ **W**   **D**

5. What does Mrs. Thomas have to do to the demand to sell 1000 gallons at the old price in September?

_____

_____ **W**   **D**

6. Name one way she could do that.

_____

_____

7. Did Mrs. Thomas lose money in August?

_____ **W**   **D**

I Rewrite the story in six sentences on your own lined paper.

Many great players played for the Los Angeles Dodgers, particularly in the 1960s. One very famous player was Sandy Koufax, who was an amazing pitcher. His style and speed are copied by many pitchers today.

J Rewrite the paragraph in four sentences on your own lined paper. If one of the sentences tells **why,** combine the sentences with **because.** If sentences seem contradictory, combine them with **although.**

The singers sang many kinds of songs. The singers sang mostly work songs and love songs. Most of their music was sung without instruments. Some of their music was sung with instruments. The singers started singing together in 1995. 1995 is when they finished high school. Sometimes, the singers perform in churches. Churches are all over town.

K Follow the directions.

1. Draw a horizontal line.
2. Draw a line that slants down to the right from the right end of the horizontal line.
3. At the bottom of the slanted line, draw an arrow that points down to the left.
4. Draw the muscle that will move the slanted line in the direction of the arrow.

204   LESSON 52

Lesson 52 from Comprehension B2 Workbook

Comprehension C— Lesson 45

Some activities presented in the **Comprehension C** program are extensions or reviews of skills taught in **Comprehension B1** and **B2**. Other skills presented in Level C are new to the students.

▲ Exercise 1 involves using the words **who** and **which**, a discrimination taught in **Comprehension B1** but which is now presented through the student-read script that characterizes **Comprehension C**.

▲ Exercise 2 involves analyzing arguments. Students have already been taught the rule regarding faulty causation: "Just because two things happen around the same time doesn't mean one thing causes the other thing." They now apply the rule to an argument. They are still prompted on the proof for the argument; however, starting in Lesson 46, they will be required to make up their own proof.

▲ Exercise 3 is the first presentation of evidence that is irrelevant to a stated rule. Note that the students have already been taught how to determine whether evidence is irrelevant or not. In this exercise, however, for the first time, they indicate whether or not it is possible to draw a conclusion based on a rule and the evidence that is presented.

▲ Student Book part D is an optional copying task (for students who are mechanically unskilled in writing).

▲ Student Book part E is a vocabulary test that requires students to substitute new vocabulary words for the underlined words in the sentences. For example, item 1 becomes "They <u>converted</u> their Swiss <u>currency</u> into Canadian <u>currency</u>."

> ★ The star (★) before part F in the Student Book indicates that students work parts F and G independently. The star (★) before part A in the Workbook indicates that students work all parts of the Workbook independently.

■ Student Book part F is a contradictions task that requires the students to compare the information provided by a map with the list of four statements about the map. Students identify statements that are contradicted by the map and indicate what the map actually shows.

■ Student Book part G is a passage to be read for information and is followed by five questions.

■ Workbook part A is a task in analyzing arguments that deals with the rule of faulty causation applied in Exercise 2.

■ Workbook part B involves the use of evidence. Students read the passage, indicate whether the conclusions given are supported or contradicted by the passage, and specify the sentence in the passage that contains the evidence to support or to contradict the conclusion.

■ Workbook part C is an independent variation of the **who-which** skill reviewed in Exercise 1.

■ Workbook part D is a review of two of the facts presented in Student Book part G. The students are responsible for remembering these facts.

LESSON 45

═══ EXERCISE 1 ═══

SENTENCE COMBINATIONS

1. (Have the students find Lesson 45, part A, in the **Student Book.**)
2. (Call on individual students to read part A.)
   Ⓐ What word? *Which.*
   Ⓑ What word? *Which.*
   Ⓒ What word? *Which.*
   Ⓓ What word? *Who.*
   Ⓔ What word? *Which.*
   Ⓕ What word? *Which.*

═══ EXERCISE 2 ═══

ANALYZING ARGUMENTS

1. (Have the students find part B.)
2. (Call on individual students to read part B.)
   Ⓖ (Call on a student.) Idea: *That if Joe taps home plate, he'll hit a home run.*
   Ⓗ (Call on a student.) Idea: *Because the last two times that Joe tapped home plate, he hit a home run.*
   Ⓘ Say it. *Just because two things happen around the same time doesn't mean that one thing causes the other thing.*

═══ EXERCISE 3 ═══

DEDUCTIONS

1. (Have the students find part C.)
2. (Call on individual students to read part C.)
   Ⓙ Say it. *Sharon is healthier now.*
   Ⓚ What's the answer? *Irrelevant.*
   Ⓛ Say it. *There is none.*
   Ⓜ What's the answer? *Relevant.*
   Ⓝ Say it. *Carla pollutes the air more.*
   Ⓞ What's the answer? *Irrelevant.*
   Ⓟ Say it. *There is none.*
   Ⓠ What's the answer? *Irrelevant.*
   Ⓡ Say it. *There is none.*
   Ⓢ What's the answer? *Relevant.*
   Ⓣ Say it. *Frieda doesn't pollute the air as much.*
   Ⓤ What's the answer? *Irrelevant.*
   Ⓥ Say it. *There is none.*

Student Book page 79

Student Book page 80

Student Book page 81

VOCABULARY TEST. Write **Part E** in the left margin of your paper. Then number it from 1 to 4. Write the model sentence that means the same thing as each sentence below. You have five minutes.

1. They <u>changed</u> their Swiss <u>money</u> into Canadian <u>money</u>.   converted, currency, currency
2. The <u>rule limited</u> their parking.   regulation, restricted
3. By <u>pausing</u>, she lost her <u>chance</u>.   hesitating, opportunity
4. His directions were <u>unclear</u> and <u>repetitive</u>.   ambiguous, redundant

★ Write **Part F** in the left margin of your paper. Then number it from 1 to 4.
Each square on the map below is five miles long and five miles wide. Assume that the map is accurate.
Examine the map carefully, and then read the statements below it.
Some of the statements contradict what the map shows.

• Write **contradictory** or **not contradictory** for each statement.
• If a statement contradicts the map, write what the map shows.

F-1. Not contradictory
2. Contradictory; Badger Lake is the biggest lake.
3. Not contradictory
4. Contradictory; three cities have more than 1000 people.

The symbol ● means that the city has between 500 and 1000 people.
The symbol ○ means that the city has between 1000 and 2000 people.
The symbol ⊙ means that the city has between 2000 and 5000 people.

1. Two cities in Himbole County have between 1000 and 2000 people.
2. Tea Lake is the biggest lake in Himbole County.
3. It is farther from Albert to Angler than it is from Smith to Kinshaw.
4. Four cities in Himbole County have more than 1000 people.

═══ EXERCISE 4 ═══

INDEPENDENT WORK

1. **[Optional]** (Have the students read the instructions for part D to themselves. Then give them exactly two minutes to copy the paragraph. Count as errors any miscopied words and punctuation. Deduct these errors from the number of copied words, and mark the total on the Writing Rate Graph.)
2. (Give the students exactly five minutes to do part E in the Student Book. At the end of five minutes, check the answers by reading each item and calling on individual students to read each model sentence.)

Note: Award 5 bonus points to the students who made no errors.

3. Finish the Student Book and do the Workbook for Lesson 45. (Wait.)

WORKCHECK

1. Exchange Student Book papers and Workbooks. Get ready to check the answers starting with Student Book part F. (Wait.) Put an **X** next to any item the person misses.
2. (Read the items. Call on individual students to answer.)
3. (Call on individual students to read each Workbook item and its answer.)
4. Figure out the person's points, and then return the Workbooks and papers. (Wait.)
5. (Have the students total their points and enter the total on the Point Summary Chart.)
6. Show me your work when you've finished correcting it. (Record points on your Record Summary Chart.)

Note: Before presenting Lesson 46, present Fact Game and Mastery Test Lesson 3, which appears at the end of this book.

Student Book page 82

 Write **Part G** in the left margin of your paper. Then number it from 1 to 5. Read the story and answer the questions.

> The Arabian horse is considered by many horse experts to be the most intelligent and sensitive of all horses. It is a white horse with just a few spots on its belly. When Arabians are young, they are not white, but spotted, and as they grow older most of the spots disappear.
>
> The Arabian horse was bred by the Arabs. The Arabs didn't wear armor in battle, so they didn't need big, heavy animals. The speed and lightness of the Arabian horse meant that it could perform well in battle. These horses became so important that many Arabs considered them to be members of the family and would sometimes let their horses sleep in their tents. At times, the horse stayed outside the tent and served as a watchdog, warning its master if an unwanted visitor came near the camp at night.
>
> Today, horse breeders frequently breed Arabian stallions with other kinds of horses. This breeding increases the intelligence of the line.

1. How does an Arabian horse's appearance change as it grows older?
2. Why didn't the Arabian people need big, heavy horses?
3. Why could Arabian horses perform well in battle?
4. Why do today's horse breeders breed Arabian stallions with other kinds of horses?
5. Where did Arabs sometimes permit their horses to sleep?

G–1. Its spots disappear.
2. Because they didnt wear armor in battle
3. Because they were fast and light
4. To produce more intelligent horses
5. In their tents

Workbook page 131

 Write the word **who** or **which** for each item. Remember, if the item refers to a human, use **who.** If the item refers to something that is not human, use **which.**

1. The trees ___which___
2. A cattle rancher ___who___
3. The cattle ___which___
4. A clerk ___who___
5. Siblings ___who___
6. The rooms ___which___
7. A girl ___who___
8. A girl's bike ___which___

D This lesson presented some facts that you will be tested on. These facts are:

1. **Arabian stallions are bred with other kinds of horses to produce more intelligent horses.**
2. **Arabian horses performed well in battle because they were light and fast.**

Study these facts. Repeat them to yourself. Writing these facts may help you to remember them.

END OF LESSON 45

Workbook page 130

ERRORS [ ] [ ] [ ]

★ A Read the argument below and answer the questions.

> While Isabel was in the grocery store, her car was stolen. She says she'll never go to a grocery store again.

1. What does Isabel conclude?
   (If she goes to a grocery store, her car will be stolen.)

2. Why does Isabel think that going to the grocery store caused her car to be stolen?
   (Because while she was in the grocery store, her car was stolen)

3. What rule does the argument break?
   (Just because two things happen around the same time doesn't mean that one thing causes the other.)

B Read the passage below.

> More Americans have been killed in traffic accidents over the past fifty years than have been killed in all the wars our country fought in from 1700 to 1950. Every hour, five people are killed in automobile accidents in the United States. Every nine seconds, someone is injured by a car.

• Here's a conclusion:

> **Every day, over a hundred people die in automobile accidents in the United States.**

1. Does the passage contain evidence to support the conclusion or evidence to contradict the conclusion?
   Evidence to support the conclusion

2. Which sentence contains the evidence?
   Every hour, five people are killed in automobile accidents in the United States.

• Here's another conclusion:

> **Cars are a fairly safe means of transportation.**

3. Does the passage contain evidence to support the conclusion or evidence to contradict the conclusion?
   Evidence to contradict the conclusion

4. Which sentence contains the evidence?
   More Americans have been killed in traffic accidents over the past fifty years than have been killed in all the wars our country fought from 1700 to 1950.

Some items in the list below are human. The word **who** is used to refer to those items.

Other items in the list are not human. The word **which** is used to refer to those items.

Tell whether you would use the word **who** or **which** for each item in the list below.

1. Matches Ⓐ
2. Paint Ⓑ
3. A cow Ⓒ
4. A cowboy Ⓓ
5. A bird's nest Ⓔ
6. A bird Ⓕ

Here's an argument:

> **The last two times Joe tapped home plate, he hit a home run. He should always remember to tap home plate when he goes up to bat.**

What does the writer want us to conclude? Ⓖ

Why does the writer think that tapping home plate will cause Joe to hit a home run? Ⓗ

Say the rule the argument breaks. Ⓘ

Here's how you could prove that tapping home plate doesn't cause Joe to hit a home run. Make Joe tap home plate every time he goes up to bat. If he doesn't hit a home run **every time** he taps home plate, then tapping home plate doesn't cause him to hit a home run.

When we draw a conclusion from a rule, we start with the rule. Then we add some other evidence. Here's a rule:

> **The more you exercise, the healthier you are.**

Here's some additional evidence:

> **Sharon exercises more now than she did a year ago.**

What's the conclusion? Ⓙ

Sometimes, we can't draw a conclusion from a rule. This happens when the additional evidence is irrelevant. Here's a rule:

> **The more you exercise, the healthier you are.**

Here's the additional evidence:

> **Olivia takes a lot of vitamins.**

What's the conclusion? There is none. We can't draw a conclusion because the additional evidence is irrelevant to the rule.

Here's another rule:

> **The more you drive, the more you pollute the air.**

Tell if each piece of evidence below is **relevant** to the rule or **irrelevant** to the rule. Remember, if it is irrelevant, you can't draw a conclusion. Here are the pieces of evidence:

1. **This year's cars are more expensive than last year's.**
   Is this evidence relevant or irrelevant? Ⓚ
   So what's the conclusion? Ⓛ
2. **Carla uses the family car twice as much as Amanda does.**
   Is this evidence relevant or irrelevant? Ⓜ
   So what's the conclusion? Ⓝ
3. **Frank is bald.**
   Is this evidence relevant or irrelevant? Ⓞ
   So what's the conclusion? Ⓟ
4. **Henry Ford built cars on an assembly line.**
   Is this evidence relevant or irrelevant? Ⓠ
   So what's the conclusion? Ⓡ
5. **Now that Frieda has a bike, she doesn't drive as much as she used to.**
   Is this evidence relevant or irrelevant? Ⓢ
   So what's the conclusion? Ⓣ
6. **Many English words have roots that are thousands of years old.**
   Is this evidence relevant or irrelevant? Ⓤ
   So what's the conclusion? Ⓥ

 Write **Part D** in the left margin of your paper. You have two minutes to copy the paragraph below.

> **Here are the rules for using "who" and "which." If the thing you're referring to is human, use the word "who." If the thing you're referring to is not human, use the word "which."**

80 LESSON 45

E **VOCABULARY TEST.** Write **Part E** in the left margin of your paper. Then number it from 1 to 4. Write the model sentence that means the same thing as each sentence below. You have five minutes.

1. They changed their Swiss money into Canadian money.
2. The rule limited their parking.
3. By pausing, she lost her chance.
4. His directions were unclear and repetitive.

★ **F** Write **Part F** in the left margin of your paper. Then number it from 1 to 4. Each square on the map below is five miles long and five miles wide. Assume that the map is accurate.
Examine the map carefully, and then read the statements below it.
Some of the statements contradict what the map shows.

- Write **contradictory** or **not contradictory** for each statement.
- If a statement contradicts the map, write what the map shows.

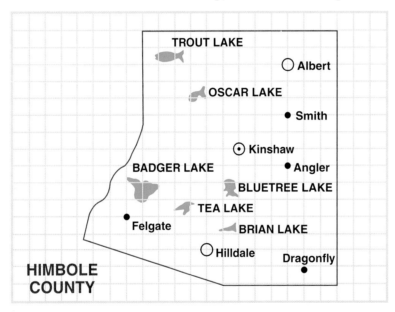

The symbol ● means that the city has between 500 and 1000 people.
The symbol ○ means that the city has between 1000 and 2000 people.
The symbol ⊙ means that the city has between 2000 and 5000 people.

1. Two cities in Himbole County have between 1000 and 2000 people.
2. Tea Lake is the biggest lake in Himbole County.
3. It is farther from Albert to Angler than it is from Smith to Kinshaw.
4. Four cities in Himbole County have more than 1000 people.

LESSON 45 **81**

Lesson 45 from Comprehension C Student Book

Write **Part G** in the left margin of your paper. Then number it from 1 to 5. Read the story and answer the questions.

The Arabian horse is considered by many horse experts to be the most intelligent and sensitive of all horses. It is a white horse with just a few spots on its belly. When Arabians are young, they are not white, but spotted, and as they grow older most of the spots disappear.

The Arabian horse was bred by the Arabs. The Arabs didn't wear armor in battle, so they didn't need big, heavy animals. The speed and lightness of the Arabian horse meant that it could perform well in battle. These horses became so important that many Arabs considered them to be members of the family and would sometimes let their horses sleep in their tents. At times, the horse stayed outside the tent and served as a watchdog, warning its master if an unwanted visitor came near the camp at night.

Today, horse breeders frequently breed Arabian stallions with other kinds of horses. This breeding increases the intelligence of the line.

1. How does an Arabian horse's appearance change as it grows older?
2. Why didn't the Arabian people need big, heavy horses?
3. Why could Arabian horses perform well in battle?
4. Why do today's horse breeders breed Arabian stallions with other kinds of horses?
5. Where did Arabs sometimes permit their horses to sleep?

82 *LESSON 45*

★ **A** Read the argument below and answer the questions.

> While Isabel was in the grocery store, her car was stolen. She says she'll never go to a grocery store again.

1. What does Isabel conclude?

   _____

   _____

   _____

2. Why does Isabel think that going to the grocery store caused her car to be stolen?

   _____

   _____

   _____

3. What rule does the argument break?

   _____

   _____

   _____

   _____

   _____

B Read the passage below.

> More Americans have been killed in traffic accidents over the past fifty years than have been killed in all the wars our country fought in from 1700 to 1950. Every hour, five people are killed in automobile accidents in the United States. Every nine seconds, someone is injured by a car.

● Here's a conclusion:

Every day, over a hundred people die in automobile accidents in the United States.

1. Does the passage contain evidence to support the conclusion or evidence to contradict the conclusion?

   _____

   _____

2. Which sentence contains the evidence?

   _____

   _____

   _____

● Here's another conclusion:

Cars are a fairly safe means of transportation.

3. Does the passage contain evidence to support the conclusion or evidence to contradict the conclusion?

   _____

   _____

4. Which sentence contains the evidence?

   _____

   _____

   _____

   _____

   _____

   _____

Write the word **who** or **which** for each item. Remember, if the item refers to a human, use **who.** If the item refers to something that is not human, use **which.**

1. The trees _____

2. A cattle rancher _____

3. The cattle _____

4. A clerk _____

5. Siblings _____

6. The rooms _____

7. A girl _____

8. A girl's bike _____

 This lesson presented some facts that you will be tested on. These facts are:

1. **Arabian stallions are bred with other kinds of horses to produce more intelligent horses.**
2. **Arabian horses performed well in battle because they were light and fast.**

Study these facts. Repeat them to yourself. Writing these facts may help you to remember them.

Comprehension Fact Game/ Mastery Test Lessons

The *Corrective Reading* Comprehension programs include Fact Games that are scheduled to occur periodically throughout the programs.

▲ **Comprehension A**—every 10 lessons

▲ **Comprehension B1**—every 5 lessons

▲ **Comprehension B2**—every 10 lessons

▲ **Comprehension C**—every 15 lessons

Most Fact Game items involve recently introduced information and vocabulary. The Fact Games provide an enjoyable format for reviewing program material and assuring that students are learning the various skills on schedule.

In Level A, students work in pairs. One student rolls dice for the whole group and tells what number the dice show. The teacher reads the item that corresponds to the number as the students follow along. One member of each pair of students whispers the answer to the other member. The teacher then tells the answer, and correct responses are tallied. Students earn 1 point for each tally.

In Levels B1 through C, students work in groups of four or five, with one student designated as the monitor. Students take turns rolling the dice, telling what number the dice show, finding the corresponding item number in the printed material, and reading and responding to the item. The monitor judges whether the answer is right or wrong (by referring to the answer key in the back of the Workbook), and awards a point for each correct answer. Following each Fact Game in these levels is a Mastery Test on the same items used in the game.

The sample Fact Game/Mastery Test lesson is presented after Lesson 20 in Comprehension B1.

▲ Item 2 is a body-systems task that requires the students to name the body system that changes food into fuel for the body—the digestive system.

▲ Items 3 and 10 are definitions tasks that require the students to name the part of speech of the underlined vocabulary words.

▲ Items 4 and 9 are deductions tasks that require the students to say the whole deduction, including the missing conclusion. Note that the conclusion in item 4 is "nothing" (the rule does not apply to the evidence), and the conclusion in item 9 involves "maybe."

▲ Items 5 and 12 are analogies tasks that require the students to say the whole analogy, including the missing word. Note that item 5 involves body-systems information and item 12 involves classification.

▲ Item 6 is a parts-of-speech task that requires the students to identify the nouns and the verbs in a given sentence.

▲ Item 7 is a body-systems task that requires the students to identify parts of the digestive system (mouth, esophagus, stomach) that are labeled in a picture.

▲ Items 8 and 11 are parts-of-speech tasks that require the students to identify the nouns and the adjectives in a given sentence.

Fact Game and Mastery Test 4

AFTER LESSON 20

FACT GAME SCORECARD

1	2	3	4	5	6	7	8	9	10
11	12	13	14	15	16	17	18	19	20
21	22	23	24	25	26	27	28	29	30

FG	MT	BONUS	TOTAL

2. Name the body system that changes food into fuel for the body.   digestive system

3. Name the part of speech for each underlined word.
   a. The selective man spent an hour choosing a tie.   adjective
   b. She was pleased with her selection.   noun

4. Say the whole deduction.
   Living things need water.
   A rock is not a living thing.

   So, __nothing_____.

5. Say the whole analogy.
   Stomach is to digestive

   as femur is to __skeletal_____.

6. **His brother was washing dishes.**
   a. What are the nouns?   brother, dishes
   b. What's the verb?   was washing

7. Name the body part shown by each letter in the picture.

   B mouth

   C esophagus

   A stomach

8. **A bus was stuck in the deep snow.**
   a. What are the nouns? bus, snow
   b. What are the adjectives? a, the, deep

9. Say the whole deduction.
   Most birds can fly.
   An ostrich is a bird.

   So, __maybe an ostrich can fly_____.

10. Name the part of speech for each underlined word.
    a. They constructed a tool shed.   verb
    b. She listened to the teacher's constructive advice.   adjective

11. **My father selected a red tie and some black socks.**
    a. What are the nouns?   father, tie, socks
    b. What are the adjectives? My, a, red, some, black

12. Say the whole analogy.
    Cup is to containers

    as hammer is to __tools_____.

FACT GAME AND MASTERY TEST 4

After Lesson 20

Note: Before beginning Lesson 21, present this Fact Game and Mastery Test lesson. You will need a pair of dice for every four or five students. Each student needs a pencil and Workbook.

FACT GAME

EXERCISE 1

1. (Divide the students into groups of four or five. Assign one player in each group to be the monitor. Set the groups at different tables with a pair of dice.)
2. (Direct the players to open their Workbooks to page 228. Direct the monitors to open their Workbooks to page 238.)
3. You have 20 minutes to play the game. (Circulate as students play. Comment on groups that are playing well.)

Points for Fact Game

1. (At the end of 20 minutes, have all students who earned more than 12 points stand up. Award 5 bonus points to these players.)
2. (Award points to monitors. Monitors receive the same number of points earned by the highest performer in the group.)
3. (Tell the monitor of each game that ran smoothly:) Your group did a good job. Give yourself and each of your players 5 bonus points. (Wait.)
4. Everybody, write your game points in Box **FG** on your Point Chart. Write your bonus points in the bonus box. (Wait.)

MASTERY TEST

EXERCISE 2

1. Now you're going to take a test on the items from the game. You'll earn 1 point for each item you get right. If you get **all** 11 items right, you'll earn 5 bonus points.
2. Take out your lined paper and number it from 2 to 12. Leave several lines between each number. (Wait.)
3. Write the answer to each item in the game. If an item says **Say** or **Tell,** write the answer instead. You have 10 minutes to complete the test. Start now.
4. (After 10 minutes:) Everybody, trade papers and Workbooks. (Wait.) I'll read the answers. Put an **X** next to each item the person misses. Do not put an **X** next to misspelled words.
(Read each item and its answer.)

Points for Mastery Test

1. Everybody, count the items the person got right. If an item has more than one part, the person must have **all** parts correct to get credit for the item.
2. Write the number of correct items in Box **MT** on the Point Chart. If all 11 items are correct, record 5 bonus points in the bonus box. Then return the papers and Workbooks.

Point Summary Chart
(Have students total their points and enter the total on the Point Summary Chart.)

Six-Lesson Point Summary
(Tell students to add the point totals for Lessons 16 through 20 and the Fact Game and Mastery Test 4 on the Point Summary Chart and to write the total for Block 4.)

Decoding Placement Test

The Decoding Placement Test is individually administered and measures each student's accuracy and oral-reading rate. Placement takes into account the student's ability to decode words in story segments and in sentences, as well as the rate at which the student reads the story segments. The test has four parts.

If you know that the student has serious decoding problems, or if you have little information about the student, begin testing with Part 1, which is a timed reading passage.

If you know that the student is a fair reader, one who has mastered many basic reading skills but who has trouble with multisyllabic vocabulary and typical textbook material, you may begin testing with Part III.

The 1999 edition Decoding Placement Test The 1999 edition of the Decoding Placement Test includes a revised Part IV test segment. The revised passage includes longer sentence structure and more varied sentence types than the 1988 Part IV test segment, and the reading rate requirement is increased. (Students who read more then 150 words per minute and meet the Part IV accuracy criterion do not need **Corrective Reading** Decoding programs.) The revised Part IV test segment better discriminates between fair readers who still need specialized reading instruction and those students who do not need **Corrective Reading.**

Preparation

Reproduce one copy of the test for each student and each tester. A reproducible copy appears on pages 198 and 199 of this guide.

Administration

Select a quiet place to administer the test. Students who are to be tested later should not observe or hear another student being tested. You will need a test form for each student and a stopwatch or a watch with a second hand. When administering the test, sit across from the student. Position the test form so that the student cannot see what you are writing on the form.

Fill out the top lines of the test form (student information). Keep this filled-out test form and hand the student a clean copy of the test.

PART I

Tell the student Read this story out loud. Follow along with your finger so you don't lose your place. Read carefully. Begin timing as soon as the student begins reading the first sentence.

Record each decoding mistake the student makes in oral reading. Mark an X on the filled-out form to show where the student made each mistake.

◆ If the student omits a word, mark an X above the omitted word.

◆ If the student adds a word that does not appear in the story, mark an X between two words to show where the word had been added.

◆ If the student misidentifies a word, mark an X above the misidentified word. Do not count the same misidentified word more than once. (For example, if the student misidentified the name "Hurn" four times, count only 1 error.)

◆ If the student cannot identify a word within 3 seconds, say the word and mark an X above it.

◆ If the student makes a mistake and then self-corrects by saying the correct word, mark an X above the word.

◆ If the student sounds out a word but does not pronounce it at a normal speaking rate, ask What word? If the student does not identify it, mark an X above the word.

◆ Do not count the re-reading of a word or phrase as an error if the word is read correctly both times.

Note: If you wish to use diagnostic procedures, you can use additional code information to indicate the type of mistake the student makes. You may, for example, write **SC** above self-corrections, **SO** above sound-out mistakes, and **O** above omitted words. You may also wish to write in what the student calls the misidentified words or what the student adds.

After each of the word-identification errors, tell the student the correct word.

When recording the errors, make sure that your copy of the story is not visible to the student. The student should not be able to see the marks that you're making.

Stop timing as soon as the student completes the story.

Enter the total errors for Part I on the appropriate line at the top of the filled-in test form. Also record the time required by the student to read Part I.

Refer to the placement schedule for Part I to determine placement or whether you should administer another part of the test.

PART II

Part II is a series of sentences that are to be read aloud by the student. You do not need to time this part of the test. To administer, present the section labeled Part II and tell the student Read these sentences out loud. Follow along with your finger so you don't lose your place. Read carefully.

Record each decoding error the student makes while reading. When the student finishes reading Part II, enter the total errors for Part II on the appropriate line at the top of the test form. Then determine the student's placement by referring to the placement schedule for Part II. Fill in the "Placement" blank at the top of the test form.

PARTS III and IV

Each of these test sections is a passage that is to be read aloud by the student and timed. To administer, present the appropriate section and tell the student I'm going to time your reading of this selection. Read out loud and read carefully. Record errors as specified for Part I.

When the student finishes reading Part III, enter the total errors and time required at the top of the test form. Then refer to the placement schedule for Part III to determine placement or whether you should administer Part IV.

When the student finishes reading Part IV, enter the total errors and time required at the top of the test form. Then determine the student's placement and fill in the "Placement" blank.

DECODING PLACEMENT SCHEDULE

ERRORS	TIME	PLACEMENT OR NEXT TEST
PART I		
22 or more	—	Administer PART II Test
12 to 21	more than 2:00	Level A, Lesson 1
12 to 21	2:00 or less	Administer PART II Test
0 to 11	more than 2:00	Level B1, Lesson 1
0 to 11	2:00 or less	Administer PART III Test
PART II		
41 or more	—	No *Corrective Reading* Placement; use a beginning reading program
8 to 40	—	Level A, Lesson 1
0 to 7	—	Level B1, Lesson 1
PART III		
15 or more	—	Level B1, Lesson 1
6 to 15	more than 2:30	Level B1, Lesson 1
6 to 15	2:30 or less	Level B2, Lesson 1
0 to 5	more than 2:30	Level B1, Lesson 1
0 to 5	2:30 or less	Administer PART IV Test
PART IV		
9 or more	—	Level B2, Lesson 1
4 to 8	more than 1:30	Level B2, Lesson 1
4 to 8	1:30 or less	Level C, Lesson 1
0 to 3	more than 1:20	Level C, Lesson 1
0 to 3	1:20 or less	Doesn't need *Corrective Reading* decoding program

SRA's Corrective Reading
Decoding Placement Test

Name _____   Class _____   Date _____

School _____   Tester _____

PART I   Errors _____   Time _____

PART II   Errors _____

PART III   Errors _____   Time _____

PART IV   Errors _____   Time _____

Placement: _____

PART I

Kit made a boat. She made the boat of tin. The nose of the boat was very thin. Kit said, "I think that this boat is ready for me to take on the lake." So Kit went to the lake with her boat.

Her boat was a lot of fun. It went fast. But when she went to dock it at the boat ramp, she did not slow it down. And the thin nose of the boat cut a hole in the boat ramp.

The man who sold gas at the boat ramp got mad. He said, "That boat cuts like a blade. Do not take the boat on this lake any more."

PART II

Can she see if it is dim?

And it can fit in a hand.

Now the hat is on her pet pig.

I sent her a clock last week.

How will we get dinner on this ship?

The swimming class went well.

When they met, he felt happy.

Then she told me how happy she was.

The tracks led to a shack next to the hill.

They said, "We will plant the last of the seeds."

What will you get when you go to the store?

You left lots of things on her desk.

PART III

Hurn was sleeping when it happened. Hurn didn't hear the big cat sneak into the cave that Hurn called his home. Suddenly Hurn was awake. Something told him, "Beware!" His eyes turned to the darkness near the mouth of the cave. Hurn felt the fur on the back of his neck stand up. His nose, like noses of all wolves, was very keen. It made him very happy when it smelled something good. But now it smelled something that made him afraid.

Hurn was five months old. He had never seen a big cat. He had seen clover and ferns and grass. He had even eaten rabbits. Hurn's mother had come back with them after she had been out hunting. She had always come back. And Hurn had always been glad to see her. But now she was not in the cave. Hurn's sister, Surt, was the only happy smell that reached Hurn's nose.

PART IV

During a good year, a large redwood will produce over six kilograms of seed, which is nearly a million and a half seeds. And the year that our redwood seed fluttered from the cone was an exceptionally good year. The parent tree produced over eight kilograms of seed that year, enough seed to start a forest that would be ten square kilometers in size. However, only a few redwood seeds survived. In fact, only three of the seeds from the parent tree survived their first year, and only one of them lived beyond the first year.

Obviously, our seed was lucky. It was a fortunate seed because it was fertile. If a seed is not fertile, it cannot grow, and about nine out of every ten redwood seeds are not fertile. Our seed also had the advantage of landing in a place where it could survive. If it had fallen on a part of the forest floor covered with thick, heavy litter, it probably would not have grown. If it had fluttered to a spot that became too dry during the summer, it would have died during the first year. Our seed landed in a spot where moles had been digging.

Comprehension Placement Test

The **Corrective Reading** Comprehension Placement Test is divided into two parts. Part I is an oral test that is individually administered. It provides an evaluation of important language-comprehension skills that are used in various reading-comprehension activities. All students should be tested on part I. If they perform according to the specified criteria, they are tested on part II. Part II is a written test that may be administered to groups of students.

Preparation

Reproduce one copy of the test for each student and each tester. A reproducible copy appears on pages 204-206 of this guide.

Each tester should become thoroughly familiar with both the presentation procedures and the acceptable responses for the various comprehension items. Tester judgment is called for in evaluating the appropriateness of responses to many items.

Administration

Select a quiet place to administer the test. Students who are to be tested later should not observe or hear another student being tested. You will need a test form for each student.

When administering the test, sit across from the student. Position the test form so that the student cannot see what you are writing on the form.

Fill out the top lines of the test form (student information). Keep the filled-out test form and hand the student a clean copy of the test.

Comprehension Part I

During part I of the Comprehension Placement Test, the student does not do any reading. You present all test items orally; the student responds orally.

Start by presenting the following general instructions. I'm going to ask you some questions. Do your best to answer them. There's no time limit, but if you don't know the answer, tell me and we'll move on to the next item. This test is not designed to grade you. It's designed to help us figure out how we can work with you most effectively.

Present the items in order, starting with item 1. If a student responds incorrectly, circle the response number that follows the item. To help you keep track, you may want to draw a line through the number when the item is answered correctly.

Items 1–3: Divergent Reasoning

These are items involving **same** and **different.** Present the instructions in a normal speaking voice. There are three response numbers for each of these items. For example, if a student names two acceptable ways that a hamburger and an ice-cream cone are different, draw lines through 1a and 1b. If the student does not name a third acceptable way, circle 1c.

You may prompt a student by saying You've named two ways that they're the same. Can you think of another way? If the student does not respond within 10 seconds after the reminder, circle the number and go to the next item.

The responses printed on the test sheet are only samples—not an exhaustive list of appropriate answers. A student's response is appropriate if it (a) expresses how the objects are the same (or how they are different), and (b) has not already been given for the pair of objects.

Note that responses are correct for the **different** items if a student mentions only one of the items. For instance, if the student says the ice-cream cone has a cone, but does not mention the hamburger, the assumption is that the hamburger does not have a cone. Therefore, the response is acceptable.

If you are in doubt about the acceptability of a response, ask the student to give a different one. For example, the student responds to item 1 by indicating that a hamburger is hot, that a hamburger has a bun, and that an ice-cream cone is cold. The last response is questionable because it is the opposite of the first response. Say Can you name another way that an ice-cream cone is different from a hamburger? Score the student's response to your question.

Items 4–6: Analogies

Item 4 is an analogy that tells where objects are found (or where the objects typically operate). Any response that accurately tells where is acceptable. For example, *lake, stream, fishing hole, ocean, aquarium,* and *under lily pads,* are acceptable.

Item 5 tells which class each object is in. Acceptable responses include *cold-blooded things, animals, food,* and *living things.*

Item 6 deals with parts of objects. Acceptable responses include *fins, tails, gills, scales, eyes,* and *teeth.*

Items 7–9: Recitation Behavior

These items test statement-repetition skill. The student receives as many as three tries at repeating the statement. You say the statement and tell the student to repeat it. If the student says exactly what you say, draw a line through the response number for that trial. If the student does not say exactly what you say, circle the number. As soon as the student repeats the statement correctly, go to the next item.

For example, if the student correctly says the statement in item 8 on the first try, draw a line through 8a and go to item 9. If the student does not say the statement correctly on the first try, circle 8a and say Let's try it again. Repeat the statement. Continue until the student has said the item correctly or until you have circled 8c.

Students must say the words clearly so they are not confused with other words. Watch for word substitutions, word omissions, and the omission of word endings—for example, saying "twenty-seven" instead of "twenty-seventh" in item 8. On the second and third try, you may emphasize the part of the sentence the student said incorrectly.

Items 10–15: Basic Information

These items test general information. For items 11 and 14, there is more than one acceptable response. For the others, however, only one answer is acceptable.

Items 16–19: Deductions

These items assess the student's ability to use deductions. Nonsense words are used in item 19. If students object to the nonsense words, remind them You can still answer the questions even if you don't know the meaning of some of the words.

Students are not required to use the precise words specified for the items; however, they should give acceptable substitutions.

Items 20–22: Divergent Reasoning

These items test the student's ability to use concepts related to **true** and **false.** Items 20 and 21 deal with descriptions that are true of some things, while item 22 deals with a contradiction (one part must be false if the other part is true).

Note that item 20c is to be presented only if the student answers 20b correctly. If the response to 20b is incorrect, circle 20b and 20c. Then go on to item 21.

Placement

Total the student's errors by counting every circled response number. Enter the total in the score blank at the beginning of the test form. Then determine the placement of the student.

PLACEMENT SCHEDULE: COMPREHENSION PART I

Total Errors	Comprehension Placement
31 or more	Place in a beginning language program, e.g., *Language for Learning*
27 to 30	Provisional placement in Level A, Lesson A*
17 to 26	Level A, Lesson A
12 to 16	Level A, Lesson 1
9 to 11	Level B1, Lesson 1
0 to 8	Administer part II

*Some students who perform in this range may perform well on Lessons A through E of Level A. If not, place them in a beginning language program.

Comprehension Part II

Part II of the Comprehension Placement Test requires students to read silently and write answers. Students should not be helped with decoding or with answers. Part II may be administered to groups of students.

Scoring

Each incorrect response counts as 1 error. If students correctly underline only part of the specified group of words in section A or B, score $\frac{1}{2}$ error.

Answer Guide

A. Words underlined:
   little plants that grow in twinglers
   wapdumpos
B. Words underlined:
   a small kerchief around his wrist
   drosling
C. 1000 gallons
   1100 gallons
   The price of milk will go up.

D.					
a. 8		**e.** 20		**i.** 4	
b. 1		**f.** 2		**j.** 13	
c. 19		**g.** 3		**k.** 7	
d. 6		**h.** 10		**l.** 16	

PLACEMENT SCHEDULE: COMPREHENSION PART II

Total Errors	Comprehension Placement
$5\frac{1}{2}$ or more	Level B, Lesson 1
2 to 5	Level C, Lesson 1
0 to $1\frac{1}{2}$	Too advanced for *Corrective Reading* series

SRA's Corrective Reading
Comprehension Placement Test

Name _____   Class _____   Date _____

School _____   Tester _____

PART I   Errors _____   Comprehension Placement _____

PART II   Errors _____   Comprehension Placement _____

PART I

Read to the student.   Circle
                                                            Errors

1. **Name three ways that an ice-cream cone is different from a hamburger.**
   One is hot. A hamburger has a bun.   1a
   One is sweet. One has meat. An ice-   1b
   cream cone has a cone. (and so forth)   1c

2. **Name three ways that an ice-cream cone is like a hamburger.**
   They are food. Each is bigger than an   2a
   ant. Both have parts. Both are   2b
   purchased. You eat them. (and so forth)   2c

3. **Name three ways that a tree is the same as a cat.**
   They are alive. Each is bigger than an   3a
   ant. Both die. They reproduce. Both   3b
   have coverings. (and so forth)   3c

4. **Finish this sentence:**
   An airplane is to air as a fish is to . . .
   Water, a lake, ocean, etc.   4

5. **Finish this sentence:**
   An airplane is to vehicles as a fish is to . . .
   Animals, food, etc.   5

6. **Finish this sentence:**
   An airplane is to wings as a fish is to . . .
   Fins, tail   6

PART I

Read to the student.   Circle
                                                            Errors

I'll say some sentences. After I say a sentence, you try to say it exactly as I said it.

7. **Here's a new sentence:**   7a
   The man on first base was not very   7b
   fast. Say it.   7c

8. **Here's a new sentence:**   8a
   It was March twenty-seventh,   8b
   nineteen sixty-five. Say it.   8c

9. **Here's a new sentence:**   9a
   Some of the people who live in   9b
   America are illiterate. Say it.   9c

10. **How many weeks are in a year?**
    52   10

11. **Listen: It has four wooden legs and a seat and a back. What is it?**
    Couch or chair   11

12. **Listen: We celebrate this day every year because it's the first day of the new year. What date is that?**
    January 1 or the first of January (In countries other than the United States, substitute a comparable local holiday.)   12

13. **Say the days of the week.**
    Students may start with any day of the week, but the days must be recited in order.   13

Circle
Read to the student. Errors

14. **What is a synonym for sad?**
Unhappy, downcast 14

15. **One season of the year is summer. Name the three other seasons.**
Fall, winter, spring (can be given in any order) 15

16. **Listen: If a dog is green, it has five legs.**
a. **Pam's dog is green. What else do you know about it?**
Idea: It has five legs. 16a
b. **Jim has something with five legs. Is it green?**
Idea: Maybe, or I don't know. 16b

17. **Listen: Some lobsters are red.**
a. **Tony has a lobster. Is it red?**
Idea: Maybe, or I don't know. 17a
b. **Mary has a lobster. Is it red?**
Idea: Maybe, or I don't know. 17b

18. **Listen: No brick walls have paint specks. Jerome has a brick wall. What else do you know about it?**
Idea: It doesn't have paint specks. 18

19. **Here's a rule. It has silly words, but you can still answer the questions.**
Listen: All lerbs have pelps.
Listen again: All lerbs have pelps.
a. **Tom has a lerb. What do you know about his lerb?**
Idea: It has pelps. 19a
b. **What would you look for to find out if something is a lerb?**
Idea: Pelps. 19b

Circle
Read to the student. Errors

20. **Listen: It is used to write with.**
a. **Is that true of a pencil?**
Yes 20a
b. **Is that true of only a pencil?**
No 20b
(Present 20c only if 20b is answered correctly.)
c. **Name two other things it is true of.**
Pen, crayon, chalk, etc. 20c

21. **Listen: It is a farm animal that has four legs, goes "moo," and gives milk.**
a. **Is that true of a cow?**
Yes 21a
b. **Is that true of only a cow?**
Yes 21b

22. **Listen to this statement and tell me what's wrong with it.**
He was fifteen years old and his younger sister was eighteen years old.
Idea: His younger sister is not younger than he is. 22

PART II

COMPREHENSION Part II

A. They planted wapdumpos, little plants that grow in twinglers.
The sentence tells the meaning of a word. Which word? _____
Underline the part of the sentence that tells what the word means.

B. His drosling, a small kerchief around his wrist, was made of silk and grosplops.
The sentence tells the meaning of a word. Which word? _____
Underline the part of the sentence that tells what the word means.

C. Here's a rule: When the demand is greater than the supply, prices go up.
Digo Dairy sells 1000 gallons of milk every day. Digo dairy has orders for 1100 gallons of milk every day.
How much is the supply of milk? _____
How much is the demand for milk? _____
What is going to happen to the price of milk at Digo Dairy? _____
_____

D. For each word in the left column, write the number of the word or phrase (from the right) that means the same thing.

a.	currency	_____	**1.**	all at once	**13.**	fittingly		
b.	suddenly	_____	**2.**	silently	**14.**	clean		
c.	ambiguous	_____	**3.**	movable	**15.**	clear		
d.	hesitated	_____	**4.**	changed	**16.**	answer		
e.	exhibited	_____	**5.**	contended	**17.**	responsible		
f.	quietly	_____	**6.**	paused	**18.**	gradually		
g.	portable	_____	**7.**	plan	**19.**	unclear		
h.	regulations	_____	**8.**	money	**20.**	showed		
i.	converted	_____	**9.**	rate	**21.**	hidden		
j.	appropriately	_____	**10.**	rules	**22.**	caused		
k.	strategy	_____	**11.**	vehicles	**23.**	slowly		
l.	response	_____	**12.**	general				

Teacher's Guide   *CORRECTIVE READING*   53

Suggested Decoding Program Sequences

Placement alternatives in SRA's Corrective Reading decoding programs and SRA's Reading Mastery series.

Some of the skills that are taught in SRA's *Corrective Reading* Decoding programs are also taught in SRA's *Reading Mastery* series. The four levels of the *Corrective Reading* Decoding programs are used primarily to teach remedial reading strategies to students in grades 3 through 12. The six levels of the *Reading Mastery* series are used to teach developmental reading strategies in kindergarten through grade 5 or grade 6, and these programs can be adapted for remedial reading instruction. Teachers familiar with both series often have trouble deciding whether to place students in *Corrective Reading* or *Reading Mastery.*

Placement decisions should be based on the following two considerations.

1 **How ingrained the student's mistake patterns are.** With an older student, the more careful sequence of the *Corrective Reading* Decoding programs is needed to extinguish older, inappropriate reading strategies and replace them with new, appropriate ones. With a younger student, the inappropriate strategies are not as firmly ingrained, and it is possible to correct error patterns more quickly.

2 **The total reading needs of the student.** If the student is deficient in both decoding and comprehension skills, the most efficient solution is a program that effectively teaches both decoding and comprehension, such as a double-strand sequence utilizing *Corrective Reading* Decoding and Comprehension programs. For the younger student in grades 2 through 4, this problem is more easily addressed than it is with an older student because (a) the younger student's inappropriate decoding strategies are not as firmly ingrained and (b) the younger student is not as relatively far behind in comprehension skills as the older student is.

Although SRA's *Reading Mastery III* is not designed as a corrective approach for either the student with poor decoding skills or the student with poor comprehension skills, the program can be used to teach both decoding and comprehension skills, after the student has learned the appropriate decoding strategies.

Once placed in *Reading Mastery III*, the student continues to practice appropriate decoding strategies and learns important comprehension skills. *Reading Mastery III* may be a good compromise approach to use with some younger students who need work in both decoding and comprehension skills, but only if those students have the necessary entry-level skills to place in the *Reading Mastery III* program.

Students in grades 3 through 12 who are poor decoders typically need more decoding practice than **Reading Mastery** provides. These students might need to complete *Corrective Reading* Decoding B1 before they will have the entry-level skills for *Reading Mastery III*, or they may need to complete **Decoding B1** and **B2** before they will have the entry-level skills for a program like *Reading Mastery IV*. If they are very weak in comprehension skills, though, they will have serious problems in *Reading Mastery IV.*

The following table summarizes placement options.

Grade	Level	Placement
2	(A) (lower)	RMI – RMII → RMIII
	(A) (higher)	FCI – RMII → RMIII
	(B1)	Regular 2nd-grade program
3	(A) (lower)	FCI – RMII → RMIII
	(A) (higher)	A – B1 → RMIII
	(B1)	B1 → RMIII
	(B2)	RMIII → RMIV
4	(A)	A – B1 → RMIII
	(B1)	B1 < B2 / RMIII
	(B2)	B2 < RMIV / C
	(C)	RMIV or C
5 or 6	(A)	A – B1 – B2 < C / RMIV
	(B1)	B1 – B2 < C / RMIV
	(B2)	B2 < C / RMIV
	(C)	C or RMV
7–12 and adult	(A)	A – B1 – B2 < C / RMIV
	(B1)	B1 – B2 < C / RMIV
	(B2)	B2 < C / RMIV
	(C)	C or RMV

○ = test placement

☐ = recommended placement

→ = final program

↗ = preferred choice of final program

A = Decoding A

B1 = Decoding B1

B2 = Decoding B2

C = Decoding C

FCI = *Reading Mastery Fast Cycle I*

RMI–V = *Reading Mastery I–V*

The circled letter shows the student's placement according to the ***Corrective Reading*** Decoding Placement Test. The boxed entry indicates a suggested initial placement for the student. The entries following the boxed entry indicate the suggested sequence the student should follow after completing the initial placement program. (Many of these sequences would not be completed in one school year.)

Grade 2.

Ordinarily, students in grade 2 are not tested for ***Corrective Reading.*** However, if a student in second grade is given the Decoding Placement Test and places in **Decoding A**, the suggested sequence is not to place the student in **Decoding A** but to place the student in *Reading Mastery Fast Cycle* instead. The choice of placement in *Reading Mastery I* or *Fast Cycle I* depends on the student's scores on the Decoding Placement Test. Lower-performing students who make 41 or more errors on Part II of the test should be placed in *Reading Mastery I* (160 lessons). Students who make between 8 and 40 errors on Part II of the test should be placed in *Reading Mastery Fast Cycle I* (70 lessons), an accelerated version of *Reading Mastery I.*

If the student's score on the Decoding Placement Test indicates placement in **Decoding B1,** the suggested placement is in a regular second-grade program. The student is not a poor decoder and does not require a remedial approach at this grade level.

Grade 3. If the student's Decoding Placement Test score indicates placement in **Decoding A** and the student's performance is low (21 to 40 errors on Part II of the test), the suggested placement is *Reading Mastery Fast Cycle I* (70 lessons), followed by regular *Reading Mastery II* (160 lessons) and *Reading Mastery III* (140 lessons).

If the student's score indicates placement in **Decoding A** but the student's performance is higher (8 to 20 errors on Part II of the test), the suggested placement is **Decoding A**, then **Decoding B1** during the same school year, followed by *Reading Mastery III* in the next school year.

Students who initially place in **Decoding B1** should complete **Decoding B1**, then begin *Reading Mastery III* (by the middle of the same school year) and complete as many lessons as possible that year.

Students who initially place in **Decoding B2** are not poor decoders and do not need a remedial approach at this grade level. The suggested placement is *Reading Mastery III*, followed by *Reading Mastery IV* in the next school year.

Grade 4. Placement options at this grade and higher grades are more varied. When two placement choices are possible, a preferred option is indicated by the top arrow in the chart.

Students who initially place in **Decoding A** should complete **Decoding A** and **B1** during the same school year, followed by *Reading Mastery III* in the next school year.

Two options are possible for students who initially place in **Decoding B1**: (1) complete **Decoding B1** and **B2** in the same school year; or (2) complete **Decoding B1**, then begin *Reading Mastery III* (by the middle of the same school year) and complete as many lessons as possible that year. Logistics may dictate that the **Decoding B1** and **B2** sequence is preferred.

Students who initially place in **Decoding B2** should complete **Decoding B2**, then begin *Reading Mastery IV* or **Decoding C** and complete as many lessons as possible that year.

Two options are possible for students who initially place in **Decoding C**: (1*) Reading Mastery IV,* or (2) **Decoding C.**

Grade 5 or 6. Students who initially place in **Decoding A** should complete **Decoding A, B1,** and **B2,** a sequence that takes longer than 1 school year. Then they should go into either **Decoding C** or *Reading Mastery IV.*

Students who initially place in **Decoding B1** should complete **Decoding B1** and **B2** in 1 year. Two options are possible the following year: (1) **Decoding C** or (2) *Reading Mastery IV.*

Two options are possible for students who initially place in **Decoding B2:** (1) **Decoding B2** followed by **Decoding C** or (2) **Decoding B2** followed by *Reading Mastery IV.*

Two options are possible for students who initially place in **Decoding C:** (1) **Decoding C** or (2) *Reading Mastery V.*

Grades 7 through 12 and adults. Students who initially place in **Decoding A** should complete **Decoding A, B1,** and **B2.** Then they should go into either **Decoding C** or *Reading Mastery IV.* (This sequence will take longer than 2 full school years to complete.)

Students who initially place in **Decoding B1** should complete **Decoding B1** and **B2.** Two options are possible the following year: (1) **Decoding C** or (2) *Reading Mastery IV.* (This sequence will take 2 full school years to complete.)

Two options are possible for students who initially place in **Decoding B2:** (1) **Decoding B2** followed by **Decoding C** or (2) **Decoding B2** followed by *Reading Mastery IV.*

Two options are possible for students who initially place in **Decoding C:** (1) **Decoding C** or (2) *Reading Mastery V.*

Students whose home language is other than English or students with serious language deficits. Neither the *Corrective Reading* Decoding programs nor the *Reading Mastery* series is intended for students who do not speak and understand English. *Corrective Reading* Decoding programs are appropriate for students who speak and understand at least easy, conversational English and whose scores on the *Corrective Reading* Decoding Placement Test indicate that they belong in one of the programs. The programs are not meant to be used with students who do not speak any English or whose grasp of English is quite weak.

Similarly, the *Corrective Reading* Decoding programs and the *Reading Mastery* series are not appropriate for students whose lack of comprehension skills prevents them from understanding most words or the details in stories they read.

Students whose home language is other than English and students in grades 2 or 3 with serious language concept deficiencies should be placed in SRA's *Language for Learning* (or *DISTAR Language 1),* an oral language program. Ideally, the *Language for Learning* program would be taught along with *Reading Mastery Fast Cycle.* Students should first become proficient in at least the first 60 lessons of *Language for Learning* before any reading instruction in *Reading Mastery Fast Cycle* is introduced. Once reading instruction begins, the students should receive a full period of language instruction and a full period of reading instruction each day. Language instruction should continue for at least 2 school years.